W9-AKT-846

Squarely

Behind

THE

Beavers

W · W · NORTON & COMPANY · INC · *New York*

DISCARDED

by Philbrook Paine

Squarely

Behind

THE

Beavers

illustrated by Larry Lurin

DISCARDED

COPYRIGHT © 1963 BY W. W. NORTON & COMPANY, INC.

FIRST EDITION

Portions of this book have appeared in *The New Hampshire Sunday News* and *New Hampshire Profiles*. The author is grateful for permission to reprint articles that have appeared in those publications. Much of chapter six appeared in *The Reader's Digest* as "The Horse That Bit Everything," Copyright 1950 by The Reader's Digest Association, Inc. Condensed from *The New Hampshire Sunday News*.

Library of Congress Catalog Card No. 63-15875

All Rights Reserved

Published simultaneously in the Dominion of Canada
by George J. McLeod Limited, Toronto

PRINTED IN THE UNITED STATES OF AMERICA
FOR THE PUBLISHERS BY THE VAIL-BALLOU PRESS

1 2 3 4 5 6 7 8 9

818

to my wife Serena,
a city girl who learned to love New Hampshire,
too

Contents

Contents

O N the following pages I have
purposely avoided using statistics about New Hampshire. As a journalist I never bother with these very
much, anyway. They only tend to be-
fuddle the writer.

But for a clue, I will state that
New Hampshire is located in the
northeast section of New England and
is surrounded by Maine, Canada, Vermont, Massachusetts, and the Atlantic
Ocean.

The village of Durham is situated
in the southeast area of the state and
contains, among other things, the State
University.

Introduction

The old homestead which appears
frequently under the name of Shankhassick overlooks the Oyster river on a
section of the town known as Durham
Point, formerly called Lubberland.

Beyond these few facts, which can
be gleaned from any geography book or
local service station attendant, no true
New Hampshireman would care to
commit himself.

Philbrook Paine

Shankhassick Farm
Durham, New Hampshire

Squarely

Behind

THE

Beavers

FROM MODERN American fiction I get the impression that there are some men in New York, Boston, Chicago and Philadelphia who wear suits of grey, despise a thing called the "old rat race," commute to work from suburbs on ramshackle trains; and as a consequence swallow too many pills, drink too much, and finally plunge into Vermont or New Hampshire to write. Free at last.

This seems to be particularly true of advertising executives whose talents require larger horizons than superacidity and liver bile copy. The public relations man likewise searches for something better than the sly news release and the committee picture. I know. I was one—for exactly eighteen years, four months, twenty-three days, seventeen hours, and twelve minutes.

I figured those statistics out on my last ride home from a public relations office in Boston to a village in New Hampshire called Durham. The conductor helped with the arithmetic. At the time, I suspected that I was doing something that had probably occurred to a lot of other people. Quit the job, grab fate by the nose, and renounce the water-cooler brigade forever. But some of my colleagues were less sure. They

Good-
Bye,
Commuting

declared that it was impossible to make a living in the country. Everybody knew that. What was I going to do? Run a ski tow?

I answered these well wishers by pointing out that they had not commuted on a Boston & Maine train through hail, sleet, storm, snow, fire, derailment, overturned automobiles, and disengaged diesels as long as I had, and thus they were incapable of making a sound judgment.

As for the job possibilities, I pointed out that the state had newspapers, and that any public relations man who could get a press release about the dairy industry past a Boston editor would certainly have no trouble buffaloing a New Hampshire paper into accepting legitimate news stories.

I also had a suspicion, which has subsequently been confirmed, that newspaper reporting was a good deal more entrancing than public relations. For eighteen years I had employed a comparatively rare principle in my public relations work. This was based on the assumption that newspaper editors were more or less intelligent people who could spot a phony news release while it was still in the mailbag. Therefore, the way to make the dairy industry look good to the milk-drinking public was to release only news that had some substance to it. Or at least some human interest in it.

For example, the fact that a cow mows a strip of pasture forty feet long by twenty feet wide every day, drinks fifteen gallons of water, and eats one sickle, three carriage bolts, and one old bicycle tire each week appeals to most editors. In exchange for this cheerful news, a lot of them were willing to print a sentence or two about the desperate plight of the dairy farmers and their two-year-old Cadillacs.

This was before the heyday of the image, so we did not worry too much about that in the dairy business. All we wanted was more money for milk and more people to drink the stuff. We were never devious in our approach to public relations.

I felt that a similar approach could be made to newspaper work. So after a short interval to celebrate my release from commuter trains, offices, committee meetings, and something called the business luncheon, I drove to Manchester, the state's largest city, to interview the editor of the Sunday paper. Almost at once it became clear that the mechanics of making a living in New Hampshire were less formidable than my friends had expected. In less than an hour, I was on the payroll as a columnist and feature writer.

But that first day's chat was enormously broadening. The editor discussed the paper's policy with me.

"Paine," he said, working on two cigarettes at the same time, "we print the news as we see it. Sometimes we initiate it. That's not the same as making it up."

He lighted a third cigarette. "Editorially," he said, "we are for beavers, mothers, dogs, and fireflies. However, we are irrevocably opposed to communists, Republicans, Democrats, Massachusetts, and any splinter groups of these parties that may be found on the moon. The main thing to remember is that the paper stands squarely behind the beavers."

Well, in New Hampshire, that is going a long way out on a limb and deserves commendation. Also, it was a long way from a public relations office where every word was carefully weighed to see that it offended no one. If I could stand the gaff on the cigarettes, I could see that the new association was going to be a pleasant one.

The American public relations industry is loaded with ex-journalists who gave up newspaper work to enjoy the financial rewards that come to those who can slip free advertising across an editor's desk. Not only is the pay better, but the hours are shorter, and a good many of these are spent sitting numbly in committee meetings and conference rooms. I am apparently one of the few who reversed this process by switching from public relations to newspaper work.

During that first interview, the editor and I straightened out one decisive matter. We agreed that I did not have to drive forty miles each day to sit in a clattering newsroom in order to write my stuff and drink Cokes from the machine. We used up a couple of packs of cigarettes over this, but when they were gone, it had been decided that I would submit suggestions to him by telephone on Tuesday mornings, receive his approval, and then go forth to gather my material.

This gave me a day to get the story, take photographs, and assemble the facts, if any. Then on Thursdays, I untangled my notes, wrote six pages, cleaned out my camera case, prepared the captions, and sent the piece off to Manchester by mail.

The system has worked admirably ever since. My new editor had long before grown weary of trying to think up story possibilities for that insatiable first page, second section. Thus, he was happy to have an eager newcomer on the staff.

There seemed to be feature stories everywhere I looked. Appropriately enough, the first one I did was on beavers. As I have related, the editor had stated his position on beavers plainly in our first interview, and I had gotten the message.

In the middle of February with three feet of snow on the ground, I actually located some beavers. They were in a brook at Nottingham, carrying on an engineering business with their usual skill and tenacity. Then I found a man who trapped them. With beginner's luck, I went with him on snowshoes one morning and got pictures of two of the animals after they had been taken out of traps.

A check with the Fish and Game Department on the rapidly expanding beaver population in the state, plus some native wit from the trapper, filled out the story. I think the editor was impressed. It had probably been some time since a feature writer on that paper had donned snowshoes to get the "big story."

Then I rode a lobster boat off of the Isles of Shoals on a wintry day with the temperature standing at fifteen degrees above zero. I got fine pictures, and the feature must have made all New Hampshire lobstermen feel like heroes. Actually, we had a pretty good time despite the cold, boiling lobsters in the engine room and kidding about the fish and game laws as they related to the legal length of a lobster's body.

During those first months I went in for the outdoor type of story. I climbed Mt. Madison in the White Mountains for a feature on the Appalachian Mountain Club huts, and nearly expired. Thirty years earlier, I had been able to carry a hundred-pound pack up the same trail in the morning and return for another one in the afternoon.

I visited fire towers to sound out the wardens on their lonely lives, only to discover that they were visited by nearly six hundred persons a week in good weather. However, when they turned up in my feature, I suppressed these facts. They were still lonely.

The Coast Guard was good for half a dozen stories. They, too, were lonely as they kept the White Island lighthouse burning brightly at the Isles of Shoals. They were lonely and heroic on their eighty-five-foot cutter, patrolling the barren New Hampshire shores. Semper Paratus. We tied up at Cape Porpoise, Maine, and were deluged by visitors. That evening, for the benefit of the newspaperman on board, the lonely crew steamed down to Hampton Beach and set off a hundred pounds of overage pyrotechnics. We could see the lights of Rye and Hampton plainly. Even car headlights were visible on the shore road. But there we sat, sending up shower after shower of distress signals into the night air less than three miles away.

Possibly, if we had set the boat afire somebody might have noticed us, but certainly no one was concerned about our distress flares that night. Still lonely, we went into Gosport harbor at the Shoals and tied up. Later on, when I was writing the story, I did not mention the overage signals for fear the news might alarm our local yachtsmen.

As the paper's waterfront reporter, I went out with the Portsmouth tugs. I watched while a taciturn pilot steered an English cable-laying ship down the tortuous Piscataqua River. He was likewise lonely and brave. I stuck to this conclusion even after he had turned the ship completely around in the narrowest part of the stream and had been compelled to start over again. The tugboat skippers were lonely and brave, too, although they went home every evening.

While I was on this lonely kick, I arranged to do a feature on the Portsmouth Naval Prison. The inmates were obviously lonely, though not brave. The first thing I discovered was that the great jail was no longer called a naval prison. It was the Retraining Command. The commandant gave me the works. I ate the same food as the prisoners did, and it was pretty good. An official photographer accompanied us on our tour, and when his flashbulb failed to go off three times in a row, and the commandant was growing purple, I showed him how to wet the bulb with his tongue.

But the cells were depressing, and the sight of men coming to attention and remaining motionless while we passed made me feel uncomfortable. A lot of the inmates were kids;

sailors who had overstayed their leaves, or had taken a heart-felt poke at an ensign, or had gone AWOL after getting "Dear John" letters. On the other hand, there were some tough nuts, too. We talked to murderers, thieves, thugs, and supply officers who had been unable to distinguish between government property and their own.

After the story had been published, I forgot about it and went on to explore the lives of other lonely people. A month or two later, an official envelope came in the mail from the Navy Department. My first thought was that this fighting service, in its ponderous way, had finally discovered what had become of the supercharger that I had borrowed from a PT mother ship for our Army boat back in New Guinea during 1944. Perhaps I was one who would wind up in the Retraining Command in Portsmouth.

But this letter had nothing to do with that supercharger. It was a standard bit of public relations for any service that receives a favorable article in the press, but I was grateful just the same. It read:

DEPARTMENT OF THE NAVY
Bureau of Naval Personnel
Washington 25, D. C.

My dear Mr. Paine:
I have read with great interest your article in the August 19 issue of the Sunday News concerning the Navy's Retraining Command at Portsmouth, N. H.

From the standpoint of good reporting, your article is excellent, presenting in a clear and interesting manner the Navy's efforts to rehabilitate its young offenders.

That you made a thorough inspection of the Command, understood what you saw and heard, and carefully reported it is plainly evident.

Congratulations on a job well done.

Sincerely yours,
(*Signed*) K. Craig
Rear Admiral, USN

I sent a copy of this to the editor, but he did not acknowledge it. He preferred letters which attacked his paper, his editorial policy, and the veracity of his reporters. If a reader wrote in and declared, "You and your paper stink . . ." he knew that he was getting attention—and circulation.

For some reason, he seldom tampered with the feature section. On the front page he might be attacking the Governor, the Milk Control Board, several aspirants for public office, and two congressmen, but the feature writer was allowed to sing the praises of any state or federal service that he liked.

Only occasionally did he make objections to a story. One of these was a feature on the Internal Revenue Service at Portsmouth. I have never been sure what he hoped that I would find. Bureaucracy, mismanagement, chicanery? Anyway, I didn't find the last two, but of course there was bureaucracy. So I wrote the story straight. What happened to your income tax and check after you had deposited them in a mailbox on April 15?

The editor held the story up for a week and then printed it for lack of anything better. The next time I called him, he was in a rage, second class.

"Look," he bellowed over the telephone. "That piece on the Internal Revenue was nothing more than a press agent's job." I could hear him slamming drawers around in a search for cigarettes. "Five thousand government employees, and you couldn't find anything wrong. You couldn't have looked very hard."

His estimate of the number of people required to collect federal taxes in New Hampshire was high, and his hope that I could locate graft and corruption in a department noted for locating graft and corruption amongst the taxpayers was plainly wishful thinking. If there had been any, the Internal Revenue would surely have known how to hide it. I offered to show him where the office was, so that he could start stirring up the nest of agents. Then, as an afterthought, I made a suggestion for the following week's story.

"What about a feature on the Border Patrol?" I asked.

"Great," he said. "Good looking uniforms, a TV program, work at night, intrepid . . ."

"And lonely," I added.

"God, yes. Lonely as hell."

With any government agency, a reporter's name commands instant attention and respect. A couple of calls to the Border Patrol headquarters in Vermont paved the way for a splendid view of the agency in action along the New Hampshire-Canadian border.

I spent a day learning how to smuggle contraband into the United States. Two Border Patrol agents had been assigned to me. We staged roadblocks, we looked at secret trails, and inspected freight cars. If it were not for a highly sensitive tip-off system which the agents have established along the wild border, anybody could start a smuggling ring in New Hampshire.

For the benefit of the paper's hundred thousand readers, some of whom might have been tempted to run a little liquor across the border once in a while, I thought I should test this system, but the agent did not advise it. "I wouldn't, if I were you," he said ominously. "It could be dangerous."

I let it go at that, though I have since been curious whether it might have been dangerous for me, or for the reputation of the Border Patrol. It certainly looked easy enough.

The editor liked the story, and the Border Patrol wrote

an appreciative letter. But there were still some more government branches to cover. The next feature concerned the FBI.
My only previous experience with this efficient arm of the law
had been about ten years before. I had caught a cold and was
spending the day in bed when somebody rapped on the front
door. I heard my wife explaining that I was sick and asleep,
and would he come back later. Then she ran up the stairs, her
eyes big, and quite out of breath. "It's the FBI," she croaked
nervously.

I attempted to calm her down, and then I tried to think
of anything that would have warranted a visit from the FBI.
There had been the For Sale sign which I had put in front of
the parsonage when I was eighteen years old, but I didn't believe that would interest Mr. Hoover. I also had one dead
headlight on the car. However, that was state trooper work,
not federal. But suddenly it came to me. He wanted to ask
me about a fur neck-piece that I had bought at the east end
of the Holland tunnel a couple of years before. That was it,
for sure. The fur had been hot, stolen. And now they would
probably get me out of bed and cart me off to Alcatraz.

I told my wife to motion him in from his car out in front.
I would go peaceably. As he came up the stairs, I was wondering whether he would use his handcuffs. He was a fine looking
chap with an intelligent face, and I knew right away that he
had me spotted as an unintentional purchaser of hot furs.

He began, "I'm checking on . . ." Here he glanced at a
sheet of paper in his hand, and I almost said, "It's up in the
attic. You can have it. I'll go quietly," when he continued, "a
person named David ———. He has applied for a job with
the Internal Revenue."

After he left, I think my wife cried a little, and I had a
long drink. However, I had learned that I would never have

made a good crook. Too willing to confess.

As a reporter interviewing the FBI, the shoe was on the other foot. I rode around with a thoroughly human agent from Nashua for a day. This time he was answering the questions, not I, and I could not refrain from questioning him about something that many people would like to know. Did he watch crime shows on television?

"Oh yes," he said, "almost every night. I am always astonished by how fast those private eyes solve crimes that would have us working for months. Allowing for commercials, some of them do it in twenty-three minutes flat. Amazing."

Equally amazing was the speed with which the feature story was sent to the U. S. Department of Justice in Washington. Within ten days, I received a letter from J. Edgar Hoover, complimenting me on my ". . . interesting and graphic presentation of the assistance given local police schools by the FBI."

This, along with other thank-you notes from various federal and state agencies, convinced me of a basic human truth. Everybody is pleased to see his own activities reported favorably in the press. Even the FBI felt it was important to acknowledge a story which made that powerful arm of the law look good.

By now, I had about covered the federal agencies in the state. Such governmental departments as Soil Conservation and County Agents I took care of in my column on Sundays. So it was now time to pry into the lives of our brave and lonely state workers. I began with the State Police. After a day of stopping cars and overloaded trucks, a trooper and I finally located a stolen vehicle. This last helped the story a good deal. It would have been hard to write a piece about the State Police without coming up with a "pinch" or at least one small crime.

Most interesting to me, however, was the fact that on his two-way radio he actually did say "ten-four" at the end of his conversations with Concord, just the way they do in Highway Patrol.

Then in rapid succession, I covered the arduous lives of our Motor Vehicle Inspectors, our Fish and Game Officers, our snowplow crews, and our Civil Defense Agency. So many of these people carried red or blue lights on the tops of their cars that I became interested in determining the total number of law enforcement officers in the state who had the power of arrest. This required a couple of days' work around Concord and led to the conclusion that in due time everybody in the state would be a police officer of some sort, with a flashing red light on his automobile. Concord officials were not impressed.

Reluctantly, I now turned away from the world of police cruisers, patrol boats, and lonely vigils to the less strenuous life of Chambers of Commerce. During the postwar period, New Hampshire industry did a magnificent job of changing over from an economy largely dependent on textile manufacturing to one of electronics.

From a news standpoint, each of the major cities had a story of resourcefulness and local initiative in making the change. Nashua and Manchester were particularly notable in this area, and few New Hampshire people ever got tired of reading about these miracles.

There is some misapprehension outside of the state concerning the New Hampshire economy. Many people seem to believe that we make our livings either by farming, or by running ski tows. Actually, New Hampshire is one of the most industrialized states in the union. The departure of the textiles only served to wake up business leaders in the various communities to the need for diversification.

For six months, I reported these local success stories. In every corner of the state, I talked with Chamber of Commerce secretaries, bankers, businessmen, industrial park managers, mayors, town managers, and merchants. Almost to the last man, they were confident, cheerful, and pleased with their communities' progress. There were good photographic possibilities, too. New factories, new housing developments, new bank buildings.

When I had completed the community series, somebody sent me a suggestion about a school near Hanover. This touched off a whole new crop of features on New Hampshire's private schools. The best-known was Phillips Exeter, but the state boasted a number of first-rate educational institutions. These landed on the feature page for a couple of months, and then I had to go out and dig again.

I explored the beauty industry in New Hampshire and found the wave-set that "thinks for itself." Then I surveyed tipping habits in the Granite State. They were still ten percent. All of this was an interesting and dramatic change from Boston and the "rat race." But the high point came each week when I called my editor on Tuesdays with story suggestions.

"Well," I would start off, reading from a list, "what about the comeback of the martens in the northern part of the state?"

There would be a pause while he lighted a cigarette. "They're kind of like a beaver, aren't they?" he'd say.

"Except that they don't swim much. They live in trees. Trappers catch them by boring a hole in the trunk and then driving nails into the hole at an angle. The marten is so curious that he puts his paw into the hole and can't draw it out because of the nails."

"I'll be damned," the editor would exclaim. "Okay. Do a story on the martens. What else have you got?"

"I might go down in a submarine and see what it's like."

Explosion at the other end of the line, incoherent shouting, and then pounding on the desk. "Submarines! Newspapermen have worn out submarines going down in them for stories. No."

"How about the Mt. Washington Cog Railway?"

"Great. Terrific. Run the locomotive. Get pictures above the clouds. What else have you got?"

"Well, I might do one on the mail boat that runs around Lake Winnipesaukee. Last of its kind."

There was a groan at the other end of the line and then the sigh of a man taxed beyond endurance. I could hear the swish of matches as he got another cigarette going.

"Oh, no. Not that mailboat again."

After I had done one hundred and fifty features on New Hampshire, both of us realized that it was almost time to start over again. But by now I was a seasoned feature writer who drove happily about New Hampshire a couple of days a week and never went near an office or a water cooler. Within the limits described above, I picked my own stories and wrote them at home. I took my own photographs and kept my own files. The American Dream had come true.

Then came the Tuesday morning call when the editor and I could not seem to come up with anything. I offered a couple of suggestions which he did not particularly like, and then he had an inspiration.

"Say," he exclaimed, "I've got a dandy idea for a feature. Guess what it is? Beavers."

"Great," I said. "First beavers, then the Coast Guard, then the Border Patrol, and the FBI, and the State Police, and the glass blowers, and the dog teams, and that progressive company in Rochester."

"Now we're cooking," he said. I could hear cigarettes being lighted all over the place.

"When can you get the beaver story?"

"Why, next week, of course," I said. "It should be easier this time. I'll go out the Concord Turnpike to a place just west of the Nottingham line. Then I'll snowshoe along the logging road for a mile and turn south toward the brook. It's the elderly one with a scar on his tail that likes to be interviewed."

IN ADDITION to the feature stories, there was also the Sunday column called "Report from the Village."
That, plus an occasional contribution
to the state magazine filled out my
week. There was now time for other
things.

For years on that commuter train
I had noticed that some of the finest
pieces of fiction being written then
were those books which bore such
titles as *Five Acres and Independence*,
*You Can Grow Most of What You
Eat*, and *Go Back to the Land*.

Since the age of seventeen I have
been the world's greatest collector of
this type of American fiction. In most
cases their authors' names are obscure
and little known outside of a relatively
small and select circle of frustrated
pioneers.

My interest in the subject was
stirred by an early perception that the
four persons in Durham who might
truthfully be called our leisure class
were those who lived off the land, more
or less. These fine, free souls combined
a natural talent for extracting food
from the ground, the sea, and the
air, with a philosophic contentment
worthy of Thoreau. While the working part of the population met appoint-

Back

To

The

Land

ments and paid bills, the happy four fished from bridges, rowed up and down the salt water river to the oyster beds, stalked the woods in search of game, and otherwise exhibited a noble disdain for "making good."

They likewise tilled the soil at a measured and judicious pace. It seemed probable then that each one's entire income for a year was under four hundred dollars, and that their principal sources of food were their gardens, shell fish, smelts, game, and wild fruit. And, though they were compelled to work at intervals, they never embraced this pastime with much enthusiasm.

Frequently during my commuting era, I felt that they had a point. On that train, in the boss's office, and during committee meetings, the same thought had occurred to me. On bright spring days in Boston, I had a hard time getting the thought out of my head that composing a news release about dairymen was the long way around to farming. I had a hunch that it might be more fun to go out and till the soil.

In exchange for sitting through interminable meetings devoted to deciding the shape and size of a milk promotion piece to be sent to school children, aged eight to ten, I received negotiable American currency. I then exchanged this in Durham for beets, carrots, meat, fish, chickens, clams, oysters, school tuition, suits to go to committee meetings in, and commuter fare. A persistent voice kept asking: Why not procure the food directly?

In answer to that voice I have been experimenting off and on for twenty-five years. Some of these experiments have been termed fiascos. Others have been more successful. The history of these can be divided into three eras. The earliest was the prewar period when I still believed that it was a great thing to commute one hundred and twenty miles each weekday, and only play at farming.

Then there was the so-called middle period when I had returned from the war with a renewed determination to raise and catch food, the way the trusty four had. And finally there have been the past five years when the land and I have begun to take each other seriously. Perhaps we should examine these various periods chronologically.

The first attempt to raise food was organized in a two-room apartment on Durham's Main Street, a few months after I was married. My bride, Serena, a city girl from Boston, viewed this latent agricultural instinct with some dismay. Everything in her experience indicated that any normal person went to a store, talked things over with the proprietor, and brought the food home in paper bags. Now suddenly she was confronted with half a dozen baby chicks. Inasmuch as there was no proper chicken house that went along with the apartment, these first six were raised in the bathtub. Looking back

on it, I can see now that this was an awkward arrangement at best. One died of the pip, despite Serena's ingenious efforts to turn the electric stove into a brooder. However, the other five eventually grew to manhood and were moved outside. At night they perched on another tenant's Model A Ford roadster, but it was a makeshift deal.

At the fall slaughtering time all hands fell to in order to prepare for the approaching winter. When this was done, it became immediately apparent that not enough thought had been given to storage facilities. Consequently, two birds had to be thrown out. Thus, of the original six only three actually arrived at the table.

But it was a start. Early in 1940 something called the Have-More Plan swept into the village. The neighboring tenant whose car had made such a good perch for the chickens procured several copies of the plan. Basically, it called for the same kind of life which my four heroes of the past had been living all along. With a part-time job and a few acres, and with a sensible amount of livestock, a family's larder would be full, the moments of quiet contemplation would increase, and life would be beautiful.

The heart of the plan, unfortunately, was the family cow, but otherwise a lot of it made good sense. I intended to substitute two goats for that objectionable item, anyway. True, it did not say much about college tuition, or cigarettes, or automobiles. I guess that was left to the imagination. However, it did stress the infinite number of staples that could be raised or gathered on your own farm.

It was like honey to a bee. By this time we had moved to a more populous part of the college town and I had read the chapter "Thirty Broilers and Independence." According to the plan, these could be raised in your backyard and never touch the ground.

Admittedly, the cage that I built was a little unsightly attached to a new house on one of the principal residential streets of the village, but it was certainly a step toward getting back to the land. After thirteen weeks, the butchering took place. It was said that some of the feathers were found a mile away on the State University campus. However, it was some time before the disillusioning aspects showed up. By keeping careful records, my wife proved beyond a doubt that though I had produced my broilers for a respectable thirty-two cents a pound, similar birds were selling in a local store for twenty-nine cents.

The answer, obviously, was mass production. With the Have-More Plan growing hotter by the minute, not only with me but with friends, several of us set out on a cooperative venture. We actually went so far as to tear down a relative's old chicken house. But then World War II intervened, and the hen house was restored to its original owner.

Even during the war, however, my interest in farming did not abate much. On a river in Australia the sight of some Holstein cows grazing along the bank of a river set in motion an elaborate plan to capture one and haul it aboard our Army crash boat. I intended to demonstrate American farming methods to my Australian crew.

Unhappily the Army did not give us enough time to execute the maneuver. In looking back at it, this was sort of too bad. We might have had the distinction of being the only crash boat in the Pacific with our own fresh milk supply. It most surely would have made the Navy's eyes pop.

Notwithstanding this failure to even an old score with cows on an American warship, this interval in the Pacific did offer a man a good deal of time to think. Always in the background were those happy four of yesteryear who had fished from bridges and rowed up and down the river.

At the end of the war, I embraced the Have-More Plan in earnest. This time it was a combination of the sea, the land, and that Boston office. In a note book which I still have, I find such headings as Operation Lobster, Operation Oysters, Operation Bean, and Operating Writing. This last was a misnomer because I think even then I was spending most of my time in committee meetings trying to decide on the shape and size of that milk promotion piece to be sent to children, aged eight to ten.

Of all the operations in those early years the most successful was Operation Oyster. Our Great Bay abounds in this shellfish, and it was no trick at all to keep a frozen supply on hand the year around. There came a time when baked oysters were met with some dismay at the dinner table.

On the other hand, the lobster operation was a definite fiasco. With fifteen traps, a power boat, a license, several hundred trips to Portsmouth to buy bait, and complicated equipment for making headers, my total catch for the season was thirty-six lobsters. They were good lobsters, all right, and they should have been. They cost exactly three dollars per pound.

The headers rotted out. Some traps got caught in the piling of an old bridge and were lost. Power boats cut the buoys off others. At the end of the season I had four left. The smell of decaying fish which lobsters appear to crave made the boat useless for any other purpose. There was household criticism. A couple of years later I sold out for ten cents on the dollar.

But there were other disasters, too. Some time during these early attempts to raise our own food, I stumbled onto a pamphlet that described raspberry culture. The profits to be made from this endeavor seemed enormous. On the old homestead to which I later moved, and which we shall be hearing more about, I hired a neighbor to plow up several acres of the back field. Then I actually ordered, paid for, and planted one thousand raspberry bushes. Three of them survived the first winter.

I was gaining experience, however.

Operation Bean was more successful. Just for the fun of it that same year I planted some string beans. But, until one has observed this vegetable closely he has no idea of its lust for life. When we had preserved three hundred and sixty-five jars of them at all times of the day and night, we quit. In the succeeding months they taught us a valuable lesson. Two people cannot eat a jar of beans every day for a year.

In 1957, my wife and I moved from the village back to my old family homestead on a section of the town known as Durham Point. Serena was still dubious about the virtues of country living, but to a dedicated pioneer with hermit instincts the stage was now set for the great experiment. Everything that had gone before had been done with an eye to the eventual goal. Exprience had been a fine teacher. Instead of planting one thousand raspberry bushes, I ordered forty. Thirty-nine of them have grown into small trees and produce more fruit than the family can eat.

In this final move to the land I ruled out livestock. I recalled too well the carefree way in which the four happy hermits of my youth had gone fishing while everybody else kept regular office hours or were owned by horses, cows, chickens and pigs. Instead, I concentrated on a small garden, small berries, and what I could extract from the sea and the forests.

The first year racoons got most of my corn. The following season the peas were planted too late and failed to fill out. The next summer I couldn't make a beet grow. Moreover, a woodchuck dug a hole in my bean row and set up his headquarters there. But I did cut and eat thirty-nine stalks of asparagus. In time I hope to be able to harvest enough for the entire neighborhood.

Despite these small set-backs, though, we have not bought a vegetable from July to March since then. Each spring I throw out enough squashes and pumpkins to fill a farm wagon. Frozen stewed tomatoes are a winter staple.

Advancing age has likewise brought a more judicious approach to extracting food from the sea. Nowadays there is moderation to the number of oysters that I tong each spring and fall. I no longer attempt to dig up all the clams in Great Bay. They should be eaten as rare treats rather than staples.

For several winters now I have watched other fishermen catch hundreds of pounds of smelts directly in front of my dock on the Durham River. Sometime soon I hope to acquire a net, an ice saw, and hundreds of dollars worth of warm clothing with which to join the parade. That is certainly part of living off the land.

At various times during this long return to nature I have tried to eat fiddlehead ferns, dandelions, salt water mussels, the Great Bay crab, bufflehead ducks, and dried corn mixed with water and cooked over an open fire. Thoreau found this a satisfactory meal, but I did not. Let's just say that all of the above items are edible but not delicious.

It has been several years since I stepped off that commuter train for the last time and became seriously involved in this business of living off the land. With each passing season I acquire a new honesty about the whole subject. I know now that a family can raise or catch a large percentage of its meals on a farm in New Hampshire. I am also willing to admit that the cost of my farm tractor would more than buy food for the entire family for a number of years.

Furthermore, I am beginning to see that life has changed since the happy four of my youth rowed down the river to the oyster beds. Note that they rowed. I have to use a couple of diesel engines and an outboard motor to get there. The old-timers preserved their oysters in a burlap bag which they dropped into the river. I freeze mine.

However, I am not disheartened by all this. There probably isn't much independence on five or fifty acres, but there is a lot of joyful and rewarding work. And that is what seems to count with me. Often on spring afternoons as I sit in the sun beside the garage shucking oysters I get to thinking about that office in Boston and wondering whether they ever decided on the shape and size of that milk promotion piece that was to be sent to school children, aged eight to ten. It hardly seems likely.

I T ALWAYS astonished me while I was working on public relations in Boston how few people in the dairy industry had ever met a cow face-to-face. During those eighteen years around the water cooler, I had been forced to suppress my real opinion of the bovine tribe in the interests of office harmony. I was forced to stretch the truth about cows and their gentle natures, their unselfish desire to supply the human race with "nature's most perfect food," and their picturesqueness on Vermont hillsides.

My fairly strong feelings about cows could be traced back to my youth. No cow that I had anything to do with ever died. They did not even get sick. Yet, when I was growing up on the old Durham homestead in 1920, cows belonging to neighbors expired right and left from eating bicycle pumps and rubber inner tubes. John Page's cow caught her horns in a barbed wire fence and promptly toppled over and broke her neck. On my sister's place a mile away a cow attempted to explore the bottom of a well and wasn't discovered until the following spring.

This close familiarity with cows took place in that twilight era just after World War I when the tradition of

My
Enemy—
The
Cow

the family cow lingered on from the early part of the century. Even in 1920 the milkman was still suspect, and few people knew what to do with a surplus herd.

Today, of course, the unwanted cows would be sold to the Government and shipped to Siam where they would generate enormous amounts of ill-will toward the United States.

But previous to 1920 our four cows, Nether Craig Spicy Peach, old Mundell, skittish Horizon, and the unpredictable Venus, had been part of the war effort. The intention, as told to me, was that this merry band and their sisters would produce milk, butter, and cheese in sizeable quantities by eating hay and grass.

Then these diary products would be consumed by the civilian population of New Hampshire who in turn would gain enough strength to carry on at home, as they say. Eventually, through a long complicated process of rationalization, this would bring about the downfall of the Kaiser and restore Democracy to the world.

Anyway, that's the way my father explained it to me when I was seven. From 1917 to 1920, our Shankhassick dairy retailed milk in the village of Durham for exactly half the price of its production. Reliable Will Burroughs, the hired man, took care of the dairy, and the Hun was on the run.

When the war ended, most of the herd was sold. Will departed, and the tradition of the family cow raised its ugly head. As a result, the trusty four remained. They were Ayrshires, and with all due respect to their breed association, this type was pretty odd, to say the least. Just an average one could outrun a horse, jump higher than a gazelle, and toss a dairyman more than twenty feet with her horns. They were marked with brown and white patches, and their forward armor made the Texas Longhorn look like a runt.

Thus, it came about that from 1920 until 1924 these four misfits and I joined our lives in one long vendetta. My three brothers had intelligently discovered that their interests lay elsewhere. Father had lost interest and had returned to writing books, which was judicious in view of the cow damages that frequently had to be paid to irate neighbors with gardens.

At the age of ten anything looks possible. I thought I could tame Spicy Peach. In the parlance of the trade, she was known as a fence-jumper. While old Mundell floundered over them like a full-rigged ship striking a bar, and Horizon depended on speed and momentum to carry her over, Spicy had her own tactics. She did not admit that the fence was there. She simply walked stolidly ahead until something gave way. Venus compromised by remaining outside the fence most of the time, anyway.

In Spicy's case, a friendly neighbor thought he could solve the problem of her fence jumping. "Drag her," he said. So I dragged her, according to his instructions. One morning soon after that, I located twenty-five feet of chain and made it fast to a ten-foot log. Then just before Spicy went barrelling out of the barn and into the pasture, I tied a stout rope around her horns. Attaching the chain to the rope was not child's play, but somehow I managed it. In other words, we both survived, which was saying something.

Although Spicy had taken a considerable interest in the log and the chain, she apparently did not connect them in her mind with the rope around her horns. Once clear of the barn door, she let out a cheerful bleat and headed pell mell for the lower pasture. She covered the first twenty-five feet rapidly enough and then fetched up short as the chain snapped taut. The resulting shock would have broken the neck of any breed less hardy and robust than an Ayrshire.

But Spicy merely picked herself up from the ground, directed a new and respectful look toward the log, and set out again for the lower pasture. This time, there were only five or six feet of slack to take up. These, however, were enough to bring her to her knees, bellowing. Now, though, she had definitely established a relationship between the log and herself, so she adopted a new tack. Putting her great head down, she moved gingerly to the end of the chain and began to pull. After all, the oxen which helped build New Hampshire

had been only slightly larger than she. In a moment, she had mastered the engineering principles involved and was plodding resolutely after the other cows. That evening, when she returned to the barn to be milked, she had added two hundred feet of wire fence to her drag.

The idea was sound, however, and it was not long before she was dragging around a couple of democrat wagon wheels, and an old grindstone and parts of a windmill fan. Actually, she made a pretty sight coming up the pasture with these various pieces of farm hardware skipping along behind her. Believers as well as skeptics turned up from miles around to watch.

Then, in the spring of 1922 she got the taxes raised. At least we have always believed so. According to an ancient New Hampshire custom the town selectmen go a-viewing early in March. They view your property, find out how you voted in the previous election, and then assess you on the basis of your doughnuts and coffee.

In this particular year they viewed the house and the coffeepot and then set out to view the barn. They chose to do this from the southeast corner at about the same time that

Spicy came around the northeast end, towing her junkyard. At the sight of so much authority Spicy came to a full stop and then cut to her right. The selectmen cut to their left. The barnyard was six inches deep in spring mud.

Afterwards, my father apologized, swore that he had voted the straight Republican ticket since the age of ten, and hurled a fairly hefty rock in the direction of the retreating Spicy. But it was no good. The taxes went up the following year, but it was a long time before the town fathers came a-viewing again.

It was my belief then, and it still is, that each cow has

some endearing quality that makes her remembered long
after she has passed away by falling into a well. Mundell, the
elder, for example, was a foot-stepper. Once she had placed
her sized-twelve hoof on the human instep she went into a
trance. She lost touch with ordinary events. If she could have
managed it, she would probably have tried to get all of her
weight onto that one hoof. But she couldn't. Therefore, she
made the best of what she had. She froze.

I could kick with my other foot. I could pummel her
thigh with my fist until it turned blue. Shouts, cries, and
threats fell on deaf ears. Eventually she might forget what she
was doing, and shift her weight, but that was simply an over-
sight.

Horizon, on the other hand, made spectacular use of her
horns. Generally, it was just good, clean Ayrshire fun. Except
on those rare occasions when she got to thinking about something else, she caught me directly above the seventh rib morning and night for four years. Then she would bounce me off
the backboard a couple of times and catch me on the carom
shot. The only hope of escape lay in the fact that usually she
lost interest and went back to butting her drinking fountain.
A spirited relationship sprang up between us.

Venus, however, was never much of a problem. That was
because she preferred the open range of an area known as
Durham Point. During her so-called dry periods she went
native in this area, and only a prolonged safari on ponyback
ever brought her back in the fall. In 1923 I failed to find any
trace of her. About Christmas time my father casually asked
what had become of Venus. I said I didn't know. Then he
shook his head dubiously and declared, "I always did think
she was half caribou."

That closed the discussion for thirty years. At the end of

this unperturbed wait, a neighbor finally disclosed her fate. "Elmer shot and et her," he confided cheerfully a few summers ago. Elmer lived two farms farther down the Point road. Despite this, though, the record remained intact. No cow of mine ever died of natural causes.

Thus by 1924, my herd was down to three cows. Although Mundell was growing weary of the struggle, the other two continued to skirmish. Horizon, just now hitting her prime, had gone dry for good. Spicy had become inoperative on one spigot after a good-natured brush with barbed wire. Despite this, however, there was still plenty of milk for everybody.

Morning and night, the cream separator whined in the kitchen, and the skim was sloshed down the drain. But even in those days our milk was probably costing thirty cents a quart.

During those four memorable years the routine was constant. When the cows were let out to pasture each day in the summer, the same Ayrshire ritual took place. Every morning Spicy and Horizon attempted to squeeze through the barn door at the same instant. Until a few years ago, bits of their hides still remained in evidence on the jambs. Approximately twelve hundred times they both tried to enter the same stall. None ever entered the correct one on the first try. Their departure from the barn was often spectacular.

Spicy invariably came out under full steam, slipped, and went down on her side. She always suspected foul play, for she would glare balefully at me, dig her great horns into the nearest object, and then scramble to her feet. Having dropped behind in this maneuver, she then set about making up for lost time. Like most cowbarns, ours was paved with concrete. The slope to the door was gradual and well grooved for sound footing. Any normal breed of cows would have considered this a safe means of egress from the stable. But not Spicy.

Having lost precious seconds in the race, she then bolted for the door with her head down, only to discover that Horizon was already blocking the way. To give Spicy credit, she did attempt to stop, but her momentum carried them both into the barnyard, like coal running down a chute. It was a sight well worth seeing.

While all of this was going on, other and older agriculturists were having better luck. Farther down the road a cow stepped into a quicksand pit. Still others ate too many bolts and old shoes and expired with dignity in their stalls. Elmer, the neighbor who "et" Venus, lost one in the saltwater river. It was a time of change.

Everywhere people were beginning to see the light. Some advanced thinkers even probed the idea of selling off their family herds. When they were not immediately struck by lightning, others began to take an interest. A neighboring city had spawned a genuine dairy plant, and the milk was said to test higher than the homegrown variety. In my case, this was believable. More than once our milk came to the table after Spicy had planted her right hind hoof in the pail.

My father's slight contact with his herd occurred on Christmas Eve, New Year's Day, and the Fourth of July. On these occasions he went to the barn and gave the cows a second feeding of grain. His true interest had begun to wane when Spicy and her stablemates licked the Kaiser in 1918.

My own feelings about cow care deteriorated even further when I approached the age of fourteen. I had begun to discover something new. One day when I went to school, the prettiest girl in the room exclaimed, "Phew, who brought the cow to class?"

That did it. From then on pressure was stepped up to

get rid of the gruesome beasts. For several weeks I went to some lengths at dinnertime to point out that (1) this was 1924, (2) the family herd was passing out of the picture, and (3) I would personally walk to town each day and buy the milk.

In return my father played coy for a long time. It was hard for him to break with tradition. At one moment he would raise my hopes by saying, "I guess I'll have to go up to Epping to see Mr. Yeaton." Mr. Yeaton bought and sold cattle. But then a couple of days later he would gaze fondly at the full milk pitcher and guess that perhaps he would only let Horizon go because she was so obviously unproductive.

My spirits rose and fell with these observations. Then about a week before my fourteenth birthday the world went black. At dinner my father announced that he had looked at the problem from all angles and had decided to keep the whole herd after all.

What would we do if there was a famine, he wanted to know? With milk from Spicy and Mundell, and by eating Horizon, we could live on for quite a long time. He made his living in front of a typewriter, and we were familiar with his dire predictions. At six-week intervals he had "written his last word." Somehow, at the time, I must have missed the twinkle in his eye when he made these remarks.

Because about a week later on my fourteenth birthday the world caved in. There were no presents. I ransacked the house, but the astonishing truth was there. They had forgotten the date.

With nothing better to do, I plodded out to tackle the chores. I intended to vent my disappointment on Spicy's tattered hide. However, when I got to the barn there was an ominous silence about it. There were no sounds of clanging horns, or scrabbling hooves, or moaning animals trying to digest old doorknobs. Moreover, a closer look revealed that the stanchions were shut the way I had left them the previous evening, only then they had had cows in them.

Now, in her heyday Spicy had been able to open her stanchion by banging around with her horns until she hit the catch, but even she had never been able to close it up again. That plodding Mundell or skittish Horizon had been able to accomplish the trick was unthinkable. I ran out of the barn to take a startled look at the pasture.

It was then that I saw a note tacked to the door. "Happy birthday, son," it read. "We gave the cows away."

There have been many birthday presents since then, but none to equal that wonderful, that incredible, that joyous and eternal silence which Spicy, old Mundell, and the useless Horizon left behind them that morning.

Years later in that public relations office in Boston I came across a promotional piece called "My Friend, the Cow." It was out in the stockroom, and I had to look twice to make sure that I had read it correctly. The shock of this sentiment set me to staring out the window in solemn recollection. My eyes may have glazed over a little. Finally I shook my head sorrowfully. Whoever wrote that title, I mused, had never been clobbered by a cow directly above the seventh rib morning and night for four years. Then I returned to the water cooler.

AFTER WORKING on the Sunday paper for three years, interviewing those beavers, and having assured myself that it was possible to live in the Granite State without writing fibs in Boston about cows, my thoughts began to turn to a place in the country. By this time my wife was also looking favorably on the project. Our daughter Sally had gone off to college, and there was no longer any good reason for continuing to live in the center of the village.

Several fiascos with real estate agencies throughout the countryside had already cost a good deal in forfeited deposit money. In each case, there had been something wrong with that particular farm. One had not been on salt water. Another had been neglected too long to make any remodeling feasible. Still another had been too small.

It was getting so that I would call an agent a couple of days after making a deposit and say, "Look, that place isn't what we really want. Get me out of it. Take the deposit money and square things up with the owner. Hire a lawyer if you have to."

The real reason for these expensive phone calls, if I had stopped to

Jacks-
of-All-
Trades

analyze them, was that none of the farms measured up to the old homestead on Durham Point, where Spicy and Mundell had gamboled thirty years before. During a good part of the time between my boyhood days and 1957, the old house had stood empty. Spicy's old pasture had sprouted a magnificent growth of alder bushes. Elsewhere, various hurricanes had uprooted many of the elm and locust trees around the house, and the lawns had grown into tangled weed patches.

In the ancient house, the plumbing was archaic, the plaster had fallen in several rooms, and the electrical wiring was of the 1918 variety. The huge old barn was beginning to sag ominously on the southwest corner. Long sections of its foundation had tumbled over.

To an outsider, the whole place had begun to resemble numerous other New Hampshire homesteads which were slowly being abandoned by families who could no longer use them. The children had grown up and departed for greener pastures, i.e., city jobs.

But it was still Shankhassick, The Shankhassick of our boyhoods. My parents had named the place after the old Indian word for the river, meaning wild goose. On the hill overlooking the decaying house, my father's workshop, where he had supported the family during my youth by turning out two novels a year, stood firm and square. The last page he wrote before he died in 1925 was still in his enormous L. C. Smith typewriter, which had two keyboards.

The slow deterioration of Shankhassick had not come about because my brothers and I had forgotten about it. At any meeting of the clan, we talked of little else. Usually, these conversations ended with brave plans to remodel the house, and rent it to some faculty member at the State University. That way, we hoped, the place would at least hold its own.

My twin brother Stuart had taken up permanent residence in California by this time, so he was particularly free and easy with his advice. My brother Delahaye, on the other hand, was beginning to evince a real interest in Shankhassick that was both surprising and welcome. Since leaving home in 1921 for Andover, his horizons had always seemed to extend beyond Durham and New Hampshire. By 1957, he had become the publisher of *Fortune* magazine, a grower of Christmas trees on his place in Connecticut; and had married Nancy White, editor of *Harper's Bazaar*.

But it soon became evident that he had never really left New Hampshire, either. Or at least he had never gotten Shankhassick out of his memory. "What ever became of the old anvil?" he asked me one night while we were watching a show in New York. I replied that it was still lying behind the stone wall near the barn where he had dropped it thirty years before. He looked so relieved that I knew that he had been thinking seriously about the old place for some time.

During subsequent visits, Del and I made our plans. We would restore Shankhassick to its pristine glory. Serena and I would live in the house. He and Nancy would remodel the barn for use on weekends and vacations. As a joint venture, we would also bring back the fields, replant the lawns, construct a dock on the river, and reshingle the log cabin. Our slogan became, "Back to 1919."

The project required three years and a good bit of U. S. currency. When it was completed, he and Nancy had a barn-home of heroic proportions, and Serena and I wound up with enough bedrooms and baths to accommodate a small army. We had also constructed a four-car garage to house the stoves and old stanchions, and I had built a dock on the banks of the river that weighed precisely one hundred and fifty tons, according to Jimmy Pike, the gravel man.

The enterprise not only proved money's power over matter, but it also showed that there are no fools like middle-aged fools; especially sentimental ones.

But it was fun. My gad, but it was fun! For three years the old place swarmed with that odd and unique breed known as New Hampshire artisans. During this time, we got to know them better than our own relatives, and we came through it all with the conviction that if New Hampshire continues to produce men like them, the state will survive for a long, long time.

We found that Granite State workmen, particularly carpenters, electricians, plumbers, masons, well drillers, and painters were honest, hard-working, inexpensive, tough-minded, often exasperating, and scarce.

As a group, they were cheerful, witty, helpful, competent, and generally "coming day after tomorrow." By training and inclination, they could look us straight in the eye and promise to do a job on Monday and then disappear for three months.

We never knew where they went. One theory was that they tended to hibernate in the winter. Another painted a darker picture of gay revels in Florida while we waited for some crucial bit of construction.

The backbone of the New Hampshire remodeling business is the jack-of-all-trades. He is equally at home with plaster, wood, electricity, pipes, septic tanks, paint, and automatic chokes. For no extra charge he also acts as counselor, friend, hunting companion, raconteur, and editorial critic, if you happen to be in that line.

The building trade, as practiced here, is perhaps our finest example of majority rule. The comparatively simple problem of placing a light on the cellar stairs in an old house calls for a preliminary caucus of the electrician, the home owner, and the carpenter. The latter gets drawn into the discussion because he has already put up the wallboard and nailed it securely. He is anxious to defend his action.

As the excitement mounts, the plumbers drop their soldering torches to advance their views. This so intrigues three painters that they climb down from their ladders to join the circle. A fellow outside who is putting up gutters has a theory on cellar lights and comes inside to expound it. A wandering well driller asks for a vote.

By rights, a simple majority of ayes or nays should now be enough to locate the light. But at this moment three men from the lumber yard arrive with materials, and their opinions have to be considered. They favor placing the light at the bottom of the stairs. This novel approach throws the convention into an uproar, and discussions begin again. However, the guy with the chain saw has missed some of the earlier claims and has to be briefed on them. The home owner, who acts as chairman of the group, then sums up the various points of view and departs. It has been decided to put off the final vote until another day.

On the other hand, our building trades in New Hampshire are shot through with individualists. These lone wolves put cabinets where they should not be, and no doors where they should be. They regard blueprints with disfavor and the home owner as comic relief.

Both of these schools toiled valiantly at Shankhassick for three years, and although our bank accounts diminished, our admiration for these New Hampshire characters continued to grow. As the years progressed, however, it became more and more difficult to determine whether they or we were the characters, anyway.

Granite State workmen conform to no pattern. On one remodeling job I knew about, everybody was a college graduate. The painter on our house formerly edited and published the paper in his home town. Another was a school principal. A plumber climbed the Alps in the summer. Our electrician was an engineer from Lehigh. He just decided one day that he wanted to be his own boss. Still another plumber served on his town's executive council.

In addition to this nonconformity, a great many New Hampshire workmen are over the age of sixty-five. I have employed painters who were eighty years old. Carpenters who labor on after the age of Social Security are the rule, not the exception. A local floor-sander is closer to ninety than he is eighty. If put side by side with a younger man, he can outwork him any day.

Henry Jones, who was a jack-of-all-trades if there ever was one, installed all of the plumbing, heating, and foundation work at the farm when he was over sixty-five. He got under the porch one day and dropped a beam on his chest that would have killed a younger man. When the doctor diagnosed it as a heart attack, he hopped out of bed and came back to work.

Henry and I were in close contact for several years, but I do not recall that he ever replied to one of my questions with anything but a chuckle that seemed to indicate that he was communicating with a fool or a child. And, he was well aware of my age.

When I built my village house during the commuting days, the boss carpenter had been sixty-eight, and his helper was seventy-one. They differed frequently about the number of nails that were being used. "What's he think you are going to do with it," the helper asked plaintively one day, "Roll it over?"

It was during this early initiation into building that I tried to cut corners toward the end. I explained that the bankroll was getting slim. Both of them laughed good-naturedly and said, "Pay us when you can. We'll finish the job."

That is one reason why the unions do not find New Hampshire any pushover for organization, except in the cities.

In remodeling Shankhassick, it was perfectly natural that Del and I should hold similar views on some things, and opposite opinions on others. There was the matter of the old library door, for example. I felt that it would probably remain open most of the time, and therefore the correct way to swing it was to the left and against any piece of furniture that might be placed there. He favored hanging it from the right so that it would bang into the closet door that had been hinged the wrong way in the first place. Our wives were content to suggest that there was no right way of hanging that particular door, and the best thing to do was to nail it securely and build in shelves on the other side. We disregarded this advice.

During the skirmish, the battered old door got turned around half a dozen times in the course of resolving our differences. It was put on one way and then the other, turned over, planed down, built up, and re-hung. Finally, one day it landed on the trash pile. The aging carpenter regarded us both good-naturedly. "It appears," he said, "that we have about worn that one out." So we flipped a coin, and I won. But we should have listened to our wives. The door that replaced the old one was hung exactly right so that every time it opens, the latch scuffs the side of my wife's antique mahogany secretary.

The painter-publisher mentioned earlier picked his crew from among his friends, neighbors, and relatives, according to their need. I kept noticing that there seemed to be more and more painters around the place. I found them everywhere, from the cellar to the attic. They started to pop out of closets. The boss painter evidently noted my astonishment one day, for he volunteered the information that several of the younger ones needed the work.

This was the same painter who came to me several days later, after the new bathtubs had been installed, and said, "I hope you don't mind, but we stayed after work Friday to give Willie a bath. He had never had a bath in a real tub before."

Not long after this, he came to me with another request. He asked if I had a spare radio. I said that I did and gave him one. Then he explained the economics behind the loan.

"If you don't have a radio for painters," he said, "they get to gabbing. First one says something. Then somebody else asks, 'What?' and the first one stops painting to repeat his conversation. This calls for an answer from the second painter, who has to stop, and then the first one asks, 'What?' And, so it goes. Back and forth, 'What?' . . . 'What?' . . . 'What?' Each time they have to stop painting so they can hear. With a radio on, they get to day dreaming and listening to the music, and gabbing stops."

At the end of two years of remodeling, the carpenters and the plumbers had caught the habit. There were radios in the barn and under the house and on stone walls. Even the brush cutter flailed away to the strains of Elvis Presley. It was like a madhouse. But very sound economically.

One thing that baffled us constantly was the universal desire of New Hampshire workmen to work outside their trades. We found good carpenters pouring concrete. Smart plumbers botching some carpentry. An electrician helping to plant shrubs. A little experience showed us that we could not change this much. So we played along with that manifestation of the New Hampshire character. No matter how good a man is in his own line, he wants to master others. My brother and I could sympathize with this. We did not go around the whole three years with our fingers bandaged for no good reason. Some of the most outrageous examples of craftsmanship at Shankhassick were left there by the owners.

The best chainsaw man I know can also call square dances, butcher beef, run a sawmill, manage a herd of cows, and operate a water wheel. He could excel in any one of these callings, but he prefers to give them all a whirl. Consequently he is always twelve months behind schedule. For three summers, he promised to mow my back field until I finally bought a tractor.

During those exhilarating years of construction here, it

was my conclusion that carpenters are the most reliable. They can hit a promised appointment within a week or two. Electricians come next, provided that you can offer them some sort of challenge. If you should let it be known that you planned to place lights at the top of every pine tree in the village, they would come running. This would be novel and new, and quite a problem. You could not keep them away.

Masons are a breed unto themselves. They arrive mysteriously and work silently. Each one is obligated by some mystic tribal law to plaster over five electrical outlets per day. I have met masons who could communicate in English, but mainly they grunt and nod their heads. This may have something to do with the speed at which they work.

Plumbers, on the other hand, communicate at will. Their interests are wide and varied, embracing nearly every subject under the sun except plumbing. As a rule, they operate about twelve months behind schedule, though some reckon their visits in light years.

I got my first insight into the New Hampshire plumbing mind at my village house. I called in a plumber to hook up my new dishwasher. That was in 1947. I called again in 1951, and once more in 1954. On each occasion he could not have been jollier. He said the matter had slipped his mind. We both had a good laugh. In the meantime, of course, I had attempted to hook the machine up myself, but it leaked.

Then a new plumber came to town. He was looking for work. Within fifteen minutes after a call to him he arrived and made the repairs. It seemed almost too good to be true. It was. He left town the following week.

But there is something admirable about that first plumber. His confident assurance that everything is going to be all right sets the home owner's mind at ease. Six months ago he was coming to tighten a shower outlet at Shankhassick. Every two days I empty a pail that catches the drip in the laundry, and I expect to continue to do this for another year. Having lived a long time in New Hampshire, I do not feel very much put out about it. An older friend called a plumber in 1920, and is still waiting patiently.

There is a maxim that a man has to build three houses before he can avoid mistakes. That is not true. My village house went off without a hitch, and the estimated cost was almost exactly right. On the next house which I built to rent, the estimates were not even close to the final bill. The remodeling of the homestead can only be termed disastrous from a financial standpoint. I do not even like to talk about it.

But I learned a good deal during those three years. For one thing, I discovered that it does not make much difference where the cellar lights go. There are never enough of them, anyway. And I have learned to take the long view about construction. When the plumbers (that's right, plumbers) put in a concrete step at the back door that was solid and heavy enough to support a fifty-story building, I merely shrugged my shoulders. I figured that long after the house had gone, that step would be there to remind future generations of the Durham pyramid builders.

By the same token, the plumbing should intrigue my descendents. The old cistern has become the septic tank, the pipe that comes in at the south corner of the cellar does not lead anywhere, and the old hand pump is just a conversation piece. But everything seems to work.

During those years of building and remodeling madness, I made friends all through the countryside abutting this college town. Because any relationship as spirited and close as home owner and builder soon rises to a first-name basis, I can recall scores of these. There were Archie Crouse and his son Bumpus. Archie was a widower, tall lean, and seventy-one years old. Bumpus was no more than a kid, with the kind of a disposition that made people around him feel good. They worked as a team, and they were thrifty. If an old piece of lumber could be made to do the job, they used it instead of a new board. Long after my village home had been completed, I used to drive to Nottingham where they lived and visit with them. We would sit in the kitchen and eat apple pie which Bumpus had made, and Archie would talk about "the old days."

Jim Wilder hailed from Northwood, a town fifteen miles from Durham, and he was about sixty-five years old when we began the restoration at the farm. He was close to sixty-eight when he left. Jim was more than a carpenter. He was a cabinet maker, yet he tackled the rough work at the barn without a murmur.

His partner, Emery Bartlett, was about my age when he started on the house, and we grew old gracefully together. Emery was the practical joker. One day I saw him tucking a short piece of wire cable over the ceiling panels so that only one end showed. I asked him about it.

"Just you wait," he said. "When the electrician starts pulling this out to make his connection to the light, he'll think that we have cut the real wire. Then listen to the explosion."

All during the barn renovation, Emery and I kept a running dart game going, and I was sorry when he left. At the end of two years, he had me down a few thousand points, but I think I could have eventually evened the score if there had been anything left to remodel.

Henry Jones and Walter Dunlap were the plumbers, the

step builders, the plaster removers, and the cellar experts. Both of them were approaching sixty-five. Henry was a stickler for protocol. He told Walter one day, "I don't think you ought to call Mr. Paine by his first name. He's the boss."

"Why in name of heaven shouldn't I?" Walter replied in some amazement. "I've known Phil since he was two months old. If he don't like it, I'll give him a spanking."

Phil Davis, the Lehigh engineer, who did the wiring was promptly named Reddy Kilowatt, after the utility ads, and he remained Reddy Kilowatt throughout the whole restoration period. Phil and I had a good deal in common besides our first names. We had both quit city jobs to return to Durham and work for ourselves. This was a subject which we never tired of discussing at some length.

And there was Charlie Gardner, the Northwood painter-publisher, who made us feel that a dab of white paint on a piece of mahogany furniture was an honor which he bestowed only on a chosen few.

In looking back fondly to that period, I doubt if I could ever again assemble a crew which so aptly demonstrated the New Hampshire characteristics of integrity, cheerfulness, and competence which those men did. During those strenuous building years, I don't recall a single harsh word being spoken by any of them to me or to each other. And that is quite a test by any standards.

When the Shankhassick remodeling was completed and Spicy's old stable had been turned into a kitchen in the barn, and Charley's stall had been converted into a living room with a piano and hi-fi, I made a vow never to build anything again. So far I have kept that promise.

But the other day, Reddy Kilowatt came down from the village to relocate a light. I had almost forgotten about his idiosyncrasies. I explained where I wanted the light, why I wanted the light, and how I wanted the light. At the end of this discourse, he gazed at a pile of old lumber in the field next to the garden and stated simply: "You'll have woodchucks." I have not seen him since.

But if I should ever build or remodel a house in the Granite State again, it will be the final one. It will be a gem. All the doors will swing the right way. The lights will be in their proper places, the cellar will be dry, and all the plumbing shut-offs are going to be in plain sight in the living room where I can get at them without crawling under the foundations.

DURING this remodeling period the problem of drilling an artesian well came up. The water system that had served so doggedly since 1908 was on its last legs, and it seemed imperative that we start over again with a well that would be adequate and close to the house.

Selecting the right spot for the new well was no problem. Almost everybody who was working on the job then had the "touch." In other words, they located water by means of the forked stick, or dowsing rod. The plumber, for example, found it about fifty feet from the house in the direction of my father's old workshop. The chain sawer came upon it closer to the barn. The electrician, who had inherited the gift from his grandfather, located it under the porch. Three painters felt that it would be found behind the barn. The carpenters were content to advise "drill any damned place and you'll find water."

Soon after that, dozens of little sticks appeared in the ground within a radius of three hundred yards of the house. Eventually, however, we compromised by setting up the drilling rig approximately ten feet from the porch where nobody had put a stick.

Cut
A
Forked
Stick

At that time I was a non-believer, although I must admit that the plumber and the man with the chainsaw had actually located the old pipe that went into the house from a former water system. But I was still not convinced.

Part of this skepticism was due to a local water dowsing experience that still had some of us chuckling.

It seemed that a couple of years before, the town had elected a water dowser to the Board of Selectmen. He was not a professional dowser, but did it principally in his spare time. Even at that he would only do it for friends and neighbors. But once he was elected, everybody figured that he would be able to locate some of the water pipes that had been missing in the village for a long time.

This fellow discovered that he had the "touch" quite by accident. He got to thinking about dowsing one night before supper, so he went out into the orchard and whittled a forked stick from a Northern Spy tree and began to stalk around the backyard.

His wife, who was sitting by a kitchen window, was disturbed to see him ambling about holding this stick in his hands, but she decided to wait awhile before calling the authorities. Pretty soon she saw him stop and back up and then move forward again. The apple branch bent down, and he grew red in the face trying to hold it. But by this time he had discovered that he had the gift, so he threw the stick over the wall and came in to supper.

Later on he got to comparing notes with other part-time dowsers and he found that his "touch" was stronger than most anybody's in these parts. In fact, his attraction to water, and vice versa, was so powerful that when he passed the stick over an underground stream the bark came right off in his hands.

He did his first real dowsing job for a friend who was building a new house out in a cow pasture. The owner thought it would be nice to know where to drill for his well and be sure of getting a good supply of water without too much expense.

So one Sunday, he held sort of a water-witching day out there in the pasture. People were hacking the wild apple trees to pieces to procure divining rods for themselves. Besides the amateurs there was also a professional man who got ten dollars for the job and the selectman.

The real dowsers demonstrated how to hold the stick with both hands about shoulder high and to walk along in a straight line. Pretty soon everybody was walking around in kind of a trance, hoping to feel the stick pull down toward the ground.

There were some sheep and cows in the pasture that were kind of bothersome, but after they had got a good look at the proceedings, they stampeded off into the woods where it was nice and safe.

It wasn't long of course before the professional dowser hollered that he had located a likely spot for the well, so he marked that with a rock. Then the selectman whooped and shouted that the stick had been torn right out of his hands at a place not far from where the owner was planning to build his house. The second amateur confirmed this a minute later and said that he had felt a right smart tug at the same location.

Nobody else was getting any reaction except sore hands, so they all crowded around and waited for the professional to give his opinion. He was getting ten dollars for the job and he had to make it seem harder than it really was.

He crisscrossed back and forth a couple of dozen times and rubbed the stick and smelt the ground and looked north, east, south, and west, and then he guessed that this was the spot. He figured that it wouldn't be too good for the dowsing trade if he let it go at that, so he got out the stick again and began to make some predictions. He said that the owner would strike water at eighteen feet, and the flow would be sixteen gallons a minute except in July when it would be fifteen and one-half gallons.

People looked so pleased at this that he went on to predict that the underground stream ran north-northeast and a quarter south on a twenty-two percent grade. Then he pocketed the ten dollars and departed.

After he had gone, the two amateurs and the selectman looked at each other and went on from where he had left off. One of them declared that the professional had been wrong about the direction of the underground stream. It felt to him, he said, waving his forked stick over the spot, more like two points off the port bow and sperm at that.

The selectman took another try and guessed that the professional had been a little bit off on the flow of the water because his divining rod told him that the owner was only going to get fourteen and one-half gallons per minute in July, especially on windy nights.

By this time everybody knew that he was kidding because there isn't a divining rod made that can tell that close.

It was just as well that people knew he was kidding, too. When the owner finally brought in the well-drilling outfit and told them to drill at that exact spot, a good many people in the village took an interest. The drillers set up their rig and started pounding away. They got down to the predicted eighteen feet pretty fast, and at the end of three weeks they were down to two hundred feet and getting nothing but dust.

After a month, they started to find some moisture, but this didn't do much for the owner who was paying the bill.

People got to asking him, "How's the well coming along. Hit any water yet?"

And he would answer morosely, "No, we haven't found any water, but we've heard somebody talking Chinese."

Well, it finally blew in at two hundred and sixty-seven feet with a volume of eleven gallons per minute, except in July when it produced twenty-three gallons a minute. Most everybody was pretty much satisfied that there had been a slight miscalculation some place, but they couldn't blame it on the selectman. The most he had claimed seriously was that he had felt a tug at that place. The professional dowser, on the other hand, never did come back to see how things had worked out.

But none of this keeps people from trying their luck with a piece of apple wood. It also provides the unfortunate owner with a bitter sort of opening remark at a party. "What will you have to drink?" he asks his guests. "Water or champagne? They cost just the same."

Off and on, I had been kidding the water dowsers in my Sunday column for some time, and, as a result, had become sort of a champion to the non-believers. A young man from Albany, New York, dropped by one afternoon and said that he was preparing a book on the subject. He wanted to know what the celebrated New Hampshire authority had to say about dowsing. So I told him.

Soon after that, I received a letter from a man in Hampton by the name of Ernest L. White. He claimed that he had been fascinated by the forked stick for years, and thought that I might be interested in what he had to say. I was.

He wrote me, "I do not question a dowser's veracity or honesty or say that he is a fake. But I do say and firmly believe that the same man who locates water by holding a forked, pliable stick in his hand could just as accurately (if he so believed) locate water without the use of that theatrical prop.

"For he may be a practical and observing man and thus absorb some of the secrets of nature; or because of a sixth sense be able to 'smell' or locate water in the same way that many natives of arid lands do by sheer instinct."

After declaring that he could make the stick work by applying pressure to it, he added, "I have not the slightest doubt that the real believers make the stick work without realizing it themselves."

It was Mr. White's influence that made me disregard the sticks in the old lawn at Shankhassick and ask the well drillers to set up their rig next to the house. This may have been a costly mistake. They struck granite at one foot and banged their way down to two hundred and eighty feet during the noisiest two months' period in the history of Durham Point. Any plaster that remained in the old house fell off the ceilings. For sixty days, the great machine groaned, thumped, hammered, and roared. Every evening, the operator and I would stare moodily down the deepening hole and probe for water.

At two hundred and twenty-five feet we heard a slight trickle. The operator dropped a huge cylinder into the shaft and measured the flow. It was one gallon a minute. So he continued to whale away. From then on we began to pick up another gallon per minute for each few feet.

Then one afternoon when I showed up, I found the well driller, the plumbers, the painters, the chainsaw man, the carpenters, the electrician, and three masons standing around the rig, peering morosely down the hole.

"He's got the drill stuck at the bottom," the plumber said with some satisfaction. "He may have to move the rig over and start drilling again."

With that, the group was joined by a journalist who was getting poorer every day, and we all stared into the hole. This was not very effective because we could only see about four feet down.

There was a telephone in the house, so the operator went in to call his headquarters. After a while he came out looking more like his old self and said something like this, "Jim says to tug the outhaul over the breech block and tackle up on the drum hoist. Then tuggle the back snatch and go ahead on the sheave shoe. If that don't do it, nothing will."

So, with the help of the plumbers, the electrician, the masons, the chainsaw man, and the carpenters, he tuggled the back snatch, and presently the stuck drill came up out of the hole. "What do you think, boss?" he said to me. "Shall I keep on drilling?" By this time I had had enough.

"Look," I said, "if you ever put that drill back in there again, I'll haunt you for the rest of your life. I'll make mysterious phone calls at three o'clock in the morning. I'll scare your kids. I'll tap on your windows. In other words, put something over that hole and never go near it again. Your luck has just about had it."

He grinned good-naturedly, wiped his brow, and shut down the engine. The previous day when we had measured the flow we had been getting six gallons a minute. That was enough. I made some swift calculations. At this rate we were assured of three hundred and sixty gallons per hour, or more than four thousand gallons per day. That was a lot of water.

Only the plumber seemed dissatisfied. I think he had been rather hoping that the pounding would go on for another two or three months, and that this would teach me a lesson about dowsing. His stick still stuck out of the ground some fifty feet from where we had drilled the well.

About a year after this, the state magazine sent me to
Exeter to interview a man who professed to be a water dowser.
The editor instructed me, "Talk to him. Find out why he
thinks he can find water with an apple-tree branch, then kid
him along. But do it gently. The thing's a fake, of course, but
see if you can discover why water dowsing continues to
flourish in New Hampshire."

This was a fairly long and complicated directive from a
man whose usual order was, "Eight pages by Thursday. I'll
pick 'em up at the Shell station."

So I made an appointment and showed up the next afternoon behind a general contractor's plant on the Epping Road
in Exeter. We went through the usual mutual suspicion with
which a reporter and his subject view each other at first. But
then I listened to the following dialogue. The time was six
p.m., and the first speaker was an honest-appearing man of
about forty-three years named Richard LaPerle. The other
end of the conversation was upheld by a forked stick cut five
minutes before from a swamp elm. LaPerle indicated that
he had just located a vein of water that ran beneath a level
piece of land in back of his office building.

Said LaPerle, addressing the stick in English, "Now I
want to know how deep the water is." The forked stick remained motionless in his hand.

"Is it five feet?" he asked. The stick continued to point
skyward.

"Is it fifteen feet? Fourteen? Thirteen?" At this point the
elm turned gradually downward. "The water is thirteen feet
below the surface," La Perle said.

Then he continued, "Now we'll measure it another way.
Watch my hands closely. First, we'll locate the vein again."
He did this by walking slowly over the ground with the dows-

ing rod held in his outstretched hands. When it dipped toward the earth, he stopped and made a mark in the gravel.

"Now I'll release my grip for a moment and take hold of it again. I am going to start walking backwards. Notice that the stick no longer points downward. However, when you see it move again, the distance between that place and the mark in the gravel indicates the depth of the water."

He moved away from the spot with the stick held firmly and pointing upward. At some distance from the original mark, the stick suddenly bent forward and down. LaPerle made another mark in the gravel and then paced off the distance between that and the one made previously with his toe at the site of the vein.

"Thirteen feet," he said.

I, too, measured it with shoes that are exactly one foot long. It was thirteen feet.

"All right," said LaPerle, "now we'll see how much water is flowing through that vein. I'll ask the stick." He addressed himself to the branch in front of him. "Is it two gallons a minute?" The branch said no and remained upright. "Is it three gallons? Four gallons? Is it fifteen gallons a minute?" The stick did not move. LaPerle started with a lower figure. "Is it five gallons?" The stick dipped toward the ground. He released his hold and held the branch in one hand, casually.

"Okay," he said to me. "We've got one vein of water here. It is thirteen feet below the surface, and it is flowing at the rate of five gallons a minute."

I believed every word of it.

At this point, LaPerle called to one of his employees by the name of Harry Darby, who operated some of the heavy equipment for the company. "Harry has the touch, too," LaPerle said. "Only the rod moves toward him and backwards."

Harry cut a forked stick of birch near a wall and returned. "All right, Harry," LaPerle said. "See if there is any water here, and if there is, see how much it flows and how deep it is."

Harry grasped the branch and started walking. He soon located the vein, measured the flow and the depth, and came back to report.

"Well, Dick," he said matter-of-factly, "I would say that we had a vein right over there." He pointed to the same area where we had already found it. "And the stick says that the

water is thirteen feet below the surface, and it is flowing at about five gallons a minute." He turned to me. "Sometimes the stick comes back and hits me in the face."

I replied that I had heard that this was true in England where many dowsing rods work the opposite way from those in America, possibly because there is so much water overhead. Moreover, I was beginning to wonder what I was going to tell my editor.

Here presumably were two perfectly honest men talking

earnestly to sticks . . . and getting answers back. Both of them had been using dowsing rods for several years. LaPerle was the head of a prosperous contracting business. He got interested in digging wells because his big, expensive back-hoe machine was lying idle part of the time. But well digging makes a minor contribution to his business. Moreover, he had said to me, "I wish I were a rich man. I'd spend all my time locating and digging wells for people who can't afford a good water supply."

He makes no charge for locating water by means of the forked stick. Therefore, what would he gain by faking the dowsing act? Furthermore, when he sets out to dig a well, he tells the owner that if he does not hit water at the predicted depth and at the rate of flow predicted by the stick, he will fill in the hole and leave no bill.

I figured I would have to come up with some answers. "Is it a highly developed power of concentration?" I asked them.

"I don't think so," LaPerle said. "We'll try it again, and you can talk to me about any subject under the sun." He picked up the branch and went searching for water. At that time, the United States was having some trouble with Russia about a U-2 plane. I spoke about this and asked what he thought the results might be.

He gave his opinion, and in the middle of it, the stick dipped down abruptly. "You see," he said, "my mind was seven thousand miles away, and the rod still worked."

"Is it your blood type?" I ventured. Harry did not know his blood type. "Perhaps electrical?" They did not think so.

We went back to the office and I related to them what I had gleaned from a couple of pamphlets the night before. At one time the U. S. Government had issued a weighty bulletin called *The Divining Rod: A History of Water Witching.*

In this, the Great White Father had come to the conclusion that, "To all inquirers the United States Geological
Survey therefore gives the advice not to expend any money
for the services of any 'water witch' or for the use of or purchase of any machine or instrument for locating underground
water or other minerals."

This consumed exactly one and a half pages of the bulletin. The next forty-six pages were devoted to tracing the
history of water dowsing since the time of the Bible. Twenty-
six of these were used simply to list the better known writings
on the subject. According to these, dowsing has been used in
every country, in every age, and in every conceivable way.

There was a man in England, for example, who claimed
that he could locate fleeing criminals by means of the rod.
This was several hundred years ago. Today, Durham boasts of
one person with the "touch" who had the famous Brink's
robbery pretty well figured out before the law finally caught
up with the criminals.

Since the Government issued that pamphlet, a good many
things have come into general use, such as the mine detector,
the geiger counter, and the depth finder. The Geological Survey may have changed its mind by now about "any machine or
instrument devised for locating underground water or other
minerals."

For one thing, the location of underground pipe by means
of brazing rods is an indisputable fact. Here again, the person
must have the "touch." This "machine or instrument" con-
sists of two brazing rods, slightly more than two feet long, six
inches of which are bent at right angles to the rest of the rod.
Copper tubing is then slipped over the ends so that the rods
can turn freely.

The dowser holds the two rods horizontally in front of himself and walks over the ground. When he crosses a pipe, the arms swing out parallel to the water main. After the operator has passed over the pipe, the rods return to their original position. I saw this demonstrated at a local gasoline station by a stranger who had no idea where the gasoline pipes were located.

LaPerle and Harry and I talked for a while about these various things, but then my mind got back to my editor. By this time, I had switched from a complete skeptic to a firm believer. How or why a forked branch can be made to speak English in a matter of moments is beyond my comprehension. But I think it does. Moreover, I should have remembered to ask LaPerle to address the stick in French to see if it was bilingual. That would have clinched the argument for me.

At this point, LaPerle declared, "I think my daughter may have the answer. She told me after she had graduated from the State University last year that there is an awful lot about the human mind that we don't understand yet. I think she has got something there."

I had to agree with him. There was a lot about my editor's mind that I did not understand. For example, how was I going to explain that in less than an hour with LaPerle I had become a convert?

Then I thought of the stick. I said to LaPerle, "Ask the rod if the state magazine is going to accept a straightforward piece about water dowsing."

The water witcher looked dubious for a moment, but then he addressed the question to the stick. "Should Mr. Paine kid the whole subject?" The branch remained motionless. "Should he expose me as a fake, but do it gently?" The position of the stick did not change.

"What about reporting exactly what he saw and heard, without drawing any conclusions?" Whereupon the swamp willow dipped violently toward the ground and twisted right out of his hands.

"That's good enough for me," I said, convinced.

When I returned home I went out to the lawn where the plumber had put the stick before the well drillers had arrived a year before and scuffed ruefully at the grass. Then I gazed over at the top of the well near the porch and thought of the expensive submerged pump that was whirring away some two hundred and eighty feet below the ground.

"We'll never know for sure," I said to the cat. "If I had only listened to Henry Jones, the plumber, we might have hit water at twenty feet."

B EFORE my brother and I could
start renovating Shankhassick, we
ran into a simple, awful truth. No
member of our family during the previous fifty years had ever thrown anything away that somehow could be
stored in the house and barn, or around
them.

In the cellar there was a crock of
eggs preserved in waterglass about a
year before Woodrow Wilson went to
the Peace Conference in France. Not
far from the crock was a shelf on which
reposed cucumber pickles put down in
Herbert Hoover's time. Beside them
were several large jars of watermelon
pickle and eight or nine jars of crab-
apple jelly that pre-dated Calvin Cool-
idge's presidency.

However, the crock of green beans
preserved while Teddy Roosevelt was
alive had gone bad. But there were
four dozen home-canned tins of vege-
tables that were picked about the time
that Warren G. Harding was leaving
Ohio for the White House. When I
threw them out a few years ago, a
definite twinge of conscience made
me hesitate.

That New Hampshire conscience
has plagued my entire family since the
day we moved to Durham in 1907, and

Throw

It

Away!

it still does. Of course, I don't exactly recall those early days too well, not having made my appearance until 1910, but I can picture it pretty well from the mementoes that have survived.

For example, I know that my parents owned a privy that first year in Durham. Although a water system was installed in 1908, this sturdy white structure lingered on until the hurricane of 1938. Every three or four years it received a coat of paint along with the house. This was because, according to New Hampshire philosophy, there was no telling when it might come in handy again.

We still have some parts of that first water system. We have even more of the second. Right after World War I, progress arrived in Durham with a vengeance. The local plumber, E. A. Prescott, had a vision. In it he saw the Paine family with a sixty-foot water tower, a pump designed to hurl water to it in great gulps, and a half-ton, single-cylinder engine which produced one horsepower per hundred pounds. I am told that people used to watch entranced while my father, sledge hammer in hand, tinkered with it on hot afternoons.

I got to know that water system well. It was better built than machinery seems to be nowadays. It worked admirably until about 1940. Then the great tower was taken down, the engine went to the scrap metal drive, and the pump . . . yes, you've guessed. The pump is still in the barn, and the steel from the water tower went to my brother's place in Connecticut for use in a home greenhouse. The last time I saw it the indestructible girders were still proclaiming to the passerby, E. A. Prescott, Durham, N. H. What paint they must have used in those days!

So far, so good. The steel did come in handy. Furthermore, in the event of a great national emergency that pump

just might make the difference between life and death, though I doubt it. Even the rusty check valve may play its part. But what concerned me about this New Hampshire thrift business was, and is, our tendency to save partially-filled bags of cement that have hardened into concrete.

For instance, when it came time to remodel the barn a few years ago, I threw out a bag that contained about ten pounds of solid cement. On it was some pencil figuring that had been done by a man who allegedly had fought in the battle of Wounded Knee. He had used most of the cement in constructing a small lawn pool here about 1917.

Before we started remodeling the house it became apparent that at one time the fashion was to save old glass preserving jars. From the evidence, this era must have extended from about 1910 to 1935. There can be no other explanation. At the same time that I threw out the old crocks and the jelly glasses, I also backed a truck up to the cellar door. My neighbor, Walter Dunlap, will sign an affidavit to the effect that we filled that truck with glass. There were big jars, medium jars, and little jars. There were old mayonnaise jars and broken jars. For two days we lugged them out in barrels. Then we carted them all down to the Durham dump and pushed them over the edge.

Almost immediately I felt a twinge of conscience. Maybe I had been a little hasty. Perhaps a few would have come in handy some day. You never could tell.

On the other hand, the Paines have never taken any chances on the return of the horse. If anybody is prepared for the ultimate failure of the automobile, it is we. Old Charley's bridle still hangs in the barn. The sleighbells could be ready at a moment's notice. Should the pony return after an absence of thirty-five years, he will find his harness waiting.

Moreover, both of them will find that we have carefully preserved the mowing machine, the cultivator, the buggy, the spring-tooth harrow, and the disk harrows. In the matter of whiffletrees, we take our hats off to no one. We have single whiffletrees and double whiffletrees, fancy whiffletrees and plain whiffletrees.

To compound the difficulty, friends who have given up waiting for the return of the horse have begun to unload their surplus whiffletrees here. They bring them to parties and think that the idea is funny. But I can tell you, whiffletrees are no joke around here. We believe in them. We must.

Almost as troublesome as the whiffletrees are the great stacks of *National Geographics* that most New Hampshire people stumble over in their attics. For years we kept ours there, but now they have gone out to the barn. I got to look at one during the move. In it was an article about some natives somewhere who were so unenlightened that they did not save whiffletrees or *National Geographics*.

A year ago I built a four-stall shed that was attached to the rear of my four-car garage. On rainy nights I felt that there should be some way to get my two small cars under cover. That turned out to be good planning. I can now get one car completely into the garage, and the other half way in. This trouble can be traced directly to earlier forms of thrift.

One stall, for example, is occupied by a 1917 Franklin touring car. This machine was driven into the barn in 1931. It was parked between the surrey and the sleigh so that we would be ready for any eventuality. And, there it stayed until 1957. Now it is being restored at vast expense in case the world runs out of water. They were air-cooled, you may recall.

The stall directly opposite this one in the shed houses our preparations for the return of Spicy and Mundell. Here are boxes filled with odd parts of stanchions, drinking fountains, a broken milking stool, and the top to the DeLaval cream separator that whined in the kitchen prior to 1924. To the average onlooker much of this may seem superfluous. But, I answer critics this way: Are they as equally well prepared for a complete breakdown in the commercial dairy business?

If there is anything, however, about which the Paines have been suspicious for a long time it is the condition of the United States oil reserves. Since about 1907, apparently we as a family have felt that the only assurance of heat in winter lay not in fuel oil and furnaces, but in wood-burning stoves. Few people have ever collected them with more enthusiasm.

We have big stoves and little stoves. We have Franklin stoves and water-heating stoves. Some are shaped like cathedrals. Others resemble do-it-yourself blast furnaces. But they all use up valuable garage space, and they are getting heavier every year. By some uncanny natural law, each one has to be moved twice every twelve months. A few are beginning to show finger grooves.

Moreover, certain alarming signs have recently appeared in still another part of the garage. That cement-saving complex that reached full flower about 1918 and then appeared to subside has returned. Only the other day I noticed that we are now saving eight partially-filled bags of cement that have hardened into concrete. If this cycle follows the course of the other, we should be getting ready to throw these bags out in 1998.

The habit of New Hampshire thrift, once it has been properly instilled in a family, is hard to break. Nancy and Serena scoff at this and make pointed remarks about saving the old ice pung runners, but my brother and I have a standard reply to these jibes. By golly, we say, at least we don't save the ribbons off Christmas packages that were received in 1922. This is usually enough to terminate the discussion.

Although the barn has been turned into a home by my brother, it really has not changed in character very much. Inside the entrance are further evidences of our preparedness for anything. Two dog harnesses assure us of a pleasant time at the South Pole, should we ever go there. Zulu spears might come in handy on an African safari. The Indian papoose holder indicates our readiness to meet the redskin more than halfway. The copper washing machine dates back to 1921, and could be a blessing in the event that all modern washing machines are called in by the government. Any one of these might come in handy somewhere and sometime.

But I have a hard time convincing myself that the broken ice cream maker will ever find a place for itself in our present scheme of things. Moreover, I look with disfavor on the mast and spars of a boat that was hauled on shore to its final resting place in 1935. The rudder which we stumble over periodically likewise appears useless in view of the present boating concepts.

Then there are the trunks. Obviously our family has looked forward confidently to the eventual failure of the clothing industry since 1907. Particularly the women members. Otherwise there is no accounting for the twenty trunks that line the barn attic. These are filled with petticoats, whalebone corsets, strange feathers, bits and pieces of cloth, and an endless number of half-knitted sweaters. Like the glass jars, these were stowed away by my mother during a period that began in 1890 and continued unabated until about 1930. Neither my brother nor I have had the intestinal fortitude to take them down to the dump where they belong. Apparently we have inherited our mother's philosophy that when every thing has gone there will still be covering for the ladies.

Moreover, it appears that our thrift is motivated not only by an extremely dim view of modern industrial methods, but also by a deeply ingrained sentimental streak. This last accounts for as much junk as the first.

For example, I noticed only recently that a tray made of wood in the manual training room of the Durham grammar school in 1921 was the object which bruised my shin in the workshop.

The half-finished ship models which likewise date back to 1921 clutter up a lot of good space. The propeller from Durham's first air boat hangs from a beam in the barn. Our fur-gathering days are recalled by innumerable rusty steel traps.

On the other side of the ledger, however, it must be admitted that a lot of this "junk" has turned into antiques. Take the Franklin, for example. In 1931 it was just a homely used car. Today, I have it underinsured for three thousand dollars. A good deal of the "junk" which my family lugged home in 1912 and carefully saved is now of great interest to the Durham Historical Society.

My real gripe about our New Hampshire thrift is that it does not discriminate enough. As already stated, we save our hardened cement bags with the same enthusiasm that we do a genuine antique. We even save our old farm machinery when we know full well that the horse has gone. Yet, the curious thing is that only last year I used the spring-tooth harrow on my back field. Also, I made the old cultivator fast to the tractor and tilled my garden.

It is hard to know around here what should be saved and what should not. Friends have been known to scoff at the old anvil and forge that repose in the shed. I pay them no heed. When old Charley and the pony return they are going to have shoes. Yes, sir, and people are going to find out that we haven't given up on the horse in this family.

As a matter of fact, old Charley has never left, really. At least the memory of him never has. Thirty-five years after his demise, I recall him often. This was because he bit things.

He bit men, women, children, and dogs. He bit trees. He could wrench a barn door right off its hinges. He was the most unforgettable horse I ever knew.

Nature had endowed him with a set of great yellow fangs that were stronger than pressed steel. In spite of the fact that he chewed almost constantly the last five years of his life, he never wore them down and he never broke any.

We always thought that the cause of this insatiable hunger was psychological. Charley didn't feel wanted. While still in his prime, he found himself being replaced by my father's first Ford car. This seemed to upset him emotionally, and during his declining years he came to brood on it more and more. The one time he bit the flivver, he chose the hot radiator cap. It was the last thing he ever bit.

Charley, like the cows, was a relic of a by-passed era. In those days no one was really sure that the automobile was here to stay. Even when it became apparent to my family that the automobile could do anything a horse could except bite, he still had no place to go.

Winters he kept to himself on the sunny side of the barn. He liked hay and grain, but he was partial to oak. Not that he spurned soft woods but he always saved the oak until the last. It was hard to tell whether this habit or the Ford was responsible for his disposition, but it got progressively worse with the years.

During the last summer of his life, he bit my twin brother,

me, an Irish Terrier, a hen, a visiting uncle, and the hired man. He had worked out a ruse for himself. In a corner of the pasture there was an old oak tree of which he was particularly fond. When he wasn't biting it he would prop himself up against the trunk and wait for his prey.

To encourage deception, he would hang his head down around his knees and stare moodily at his great front hooves. Anybody seeing him would have thought, "Old white horse leaning against a tree. Nothing to worry about."

That was what Charley wanted. At the right moment he would take off with a tremendous thud of flying feet and catch his victim halfway to the fence. He had a fondness for arms, though he settled once for the terrier's tail.

It was the uncle, however, who cooked his goose. Charley should have let him go by. This was a grave error in judgment.

He caught my Uncle Ben halfway to the fence one day and gave him a thorough going over. He bit him a couple of times on the arm and once on the right leg. By the time Uncle Ben had recovered enough to crawl out of the pasture, old Charley had gone back to gnawing on his oak tree.

As soon as Ben had got himself patched up, he swore that he would get across that pasture somehow. So he cranked up the Model T Ford and ran it around to the gate and into the pasture. Then he took off past the oak tree.

Just as he had hoped, old Charley was leaning up against it, practicing his ruse. He didn't move a muscle until the Ford was halfway there. Then he lit out after it. Uncle Ben had been expecting this. He opened the throttle and sped off toward the fence.

Old Charley was surprisingly fast on his feet, and when Uncle Ben looked back he saw a great mouth about to close on his shoulder. So he abandoned the flivver and went over the fence. The Ford fetched up in a patch of juniper and came to a stop. Charley came clomping up to it, looking meaner than a rattlesnake and twice as frustrated.

That was when he bit the hot radiator cap. Naturally he let go of it prettty fast, but not before he had learned something new about Fords. This knowledge apparently did something to his spirit.

For the next day his head hung down even farther than usual, and he kept his tongue out in the air as though he were trying to cool it. However, it was easy to see that his ailment was of the mind and not the body. He didn't even bother to bite anything all day long. That was sign enough. The jig was about up.

That night, defeated by the internal combustion engine, weary at heart, and baffled in mind, he slumped down beside his oak tree and passed away.

But regardless of what else he lacked, he had pride. This became apparent the next morning. As the end neared, he had made some small effort to put his affairs in order. He had yanked in his tongue and closed his mouth. No horse could have done more.

*S*PEAKING of Fords, nothing marks the quick passage of time better than the realization that two generations of Americans have grown up since the last Model T was made. The final one rolled off the assembly line in 1927, and with it passed an era. The one that polished off old Charley was spawned in 1914.

Between that eventful day and about 1930, my family owned a succession of Model T's and Franklins. And, although I still have our first Franklin, our New Hampshire instinct for saving things let us down on the Model T's. We didn't keep a single one. Today they would be worth thousands of dollars.

There are still a few relics around, on campuses and in barns where wiser owners than we have stored them away, but for honest transportation they have just about gone the way of the dodo. Growing up in the land today is a whole uninitiated section of the population that never rode in a Model T Ford. Yet, between 1912 and 1930, flivvers were the main form of transportation in Durham, and most of the United States.

So let us old-timers refresh our memories for a moment.

Flivvers
And
Franklins

The Model T was an indestructible piece of machinery that ran on four wheels and was propelled by an engineering nightmare under the hood. Its chief virtue lay in its bulldog determination to get you there and get you back. That this frequently required patience and stamina seems to have been forgotten. The point was this: When they did break down almost anybody could make them go again. In those far-off days everybody was a fair to middling mechanic. He had to be!

There was nothing wrong with the Model T engine. It had four cylinders of considerable size that could get down and pull like oxen on a grade. Very often, however, they exhibited a streak of temperament that was surprising in anything so homely. Most of this unpredictability stemmed from a diabolical ignition system that was certainly no credit to anybody in Detroit. It had four coils that were bedded down inside the car itself, not far from the driver's feet. In operation they made a high, buzzy noise that was generally drowned out by the sound of the engine itself.

Actually, these coils were the heart and soul of the Model T. Any driver refusing to recognize their special caprices was likely to find himself walking home. The coils had to be pampered. They had things called points; and when an owner could think of nothing better to do, he "changed the points." If this did not do anything, he "changed the gap" of the sparkplugs. This friendship with the Ford's nervous system was part of the informality of driving in those days.

On the other hand, there was a certain school of mechanics who refused to coddle their cars. They found that a good smart kick to the coil box was highly effective. Many a driver was rewarded by a quick start after the coils had been soundly belted with a size twelve boot.

By far the most preposterous thing about the Model T

was its transmission. When it left Detroit, it had some high-falutin' name like planetary transmission, but always thereafter it was referred to with some heat as "them . . . bands." This was more or less a term of affection for something so monstrous that most people could not believe that it was true.

Instead of two pedals, it had three. These were jammed together in an area the size of a dinner plate, so that a large man had trouble hitting one without pushing all three. "Them bands" were down inside a metal container directly behind the engine. The space allowed for getting at them was almost non-existent, and very often small children were pressed into service when repairs were needed, which was constantly.

"Them bands" suffered from a chronic sort of ailment that announced itself with clouds of acrid smoke that poured up from below the driver's feet. When that happened, owners knew that they had burned out another set. Astute people carried spare sets and a length of hay wire and changed them on the spot. At best, though, it was a temper-warming job.

This weird transmission—in which high, low, reverse, and neutral were never too clearly defined—accounted for the Model T's tendency to chase people whenever the temperature dropped below forty degrees. The three brake bands ran in a bath of oil which thickened in cool weather. This caused a kind of stubborn reluctance on the part of the high-low band to go into neutral. Consequently, in cold climates, the Ford's natural instinct was to move off as soon as the engine started.

To prevent this, owners sometimes resorted to an expedient that not only kept themselves from being chased, but also materially improved the chances of the car's starting. This was a device that lifted one hind wheel off the ground, leaving it free to turn. Few drivers had the time or inclination to fool around with a jack. Far quicker was a chunk of oak from the woodpile. They used this as a block after lifting the rear end clear of the ground. The entire weight of the Model T was probably less than three hundred pounds on each wheel. Nevertheless, the problem of getting the oak piece under the axle called for a certain delicacy of judgment. For it is obvious that while the owner was engaged with both hands in lifting the wheel off the ground, he could not run around and shove the wood under the rear end.

Therefore, he solved the problem by leaning the chunk against the axle at an angle. Once he had lifted the wheel, the block's natural tendency was to return to its upright position, which placed it squarely under the axle housing. The tire now cleared the ground by an inch or two and was free to turn.

To arouse the engine on cold mornings was something else again. The self starter on a flivver was more of a conception than a reality. The advertisements claimed that the Ford had one, and it was no secret that there was some sort of a mechanism down on one side of the engine that made a noise. But it was mostly talk.

Batteries were not what they are today, and smart people were content to have enough "juice" to make the coils buzz. Moreover, the Model T had a proclivity toward "kicking." When this occurred, the starting mechanism disintegrated. As a result most owners depended on their cranks.

This tendency to "kick," however, was more pronounced in some cars than it was in others. A few were notorious. It was not uncommon to see two bandaged wrists in the same family at the same time.

For the uninitiated, the term "kicking" was a word to describe the obstinate desire of a Ford engine to suddenly reverse itself and start going in the opposite rotation. This happened only during the starting period, but it could be right devastat-

ing to the human wrist. Local knowledge separated those that
you could "spin" and those that you could not.

Cranking a Model T likewise set the stage for one of the
most ludicrous of human experiences. This was the embarrass-
ing situation of being chased by a Ford car. It came about at
the moment when the engine started and the rear axle simultaneously jiggled off the chunk of oak. Then the owner wished
that the Model T's well-known determination to get on with
things was less pronounced.

He would let out a cry of indignation and sprint for the
other end of the barn, with the flivver yelping at his heels.
Most generally he made it. A few escaped by hurling themselves into the grain bin. Others hid behind posts.

However, every once in a while a Model T would catch
up with a slow man. At that point there was only one thing
left to do: Leap aboard the hood and ride her through the
end of the barn like a bronco.

There were some other curious features to the Ford that

deserve recall. One was the hand brake located to the left of the driver's seat. It performed several functions. Besides the obvious one, it also served as a decisive factor in getting the car into high gear and neutral. In addition, it served as a resting place for the left foot. For this last purpose, no car ever built has come up with anything better.

Then there was that gas tank. This was placed under the front seat, only a few inches above the engine. When the supply of gas was low, the difference in height was not enough to get it to the carburetor. Consequently, Ford owners resorted to backing their cars up steep hills. It was not uncommon in those days to see three or four Fords solemnly reversing their way up a grade.

Among local owners, my father garnered some fame for overcoming this defect on a trip to a city nearby by dropping all of the tools and old sparkplugs into the tank in order to raise the level of the gasoline. The task of getting them out again, once the immediate problem had been overcome, was a matter of historical record for many years.

However, in fairness to a noble machine one superlative virtue should be mentioned. With each new car came a wrench. It was just a plain, old-fashioned Ford wrench, but it would fit any space and take off any nut. Now, some thirty or forty years later, the flivvers have gone, but most of us still have those wrenches.

Far less popular in the village, but still surprisingly numerous, was the wonderful air-cooled Franklin. This was a freak sort of automobile that rose to popularity in the twenties, but eventually succumbed to progress in the mid-thirties. Paradoxically, the characteristic that made them great also caused their downfall. Franklin automobiles were too well built. The engineers at Syracuse misjudged the wants of the

American public and designed their product to last forever. The 1917 model in my garage ran eighty thousand miles with fewer repairs than I give my lawn mower in a season.

The Franklin's air-cooled engine set them apart from other cars. The fact that they had no radiators caused their owners to feel slightly superior to those unfortunates who messed around with water and anti-freeze. Even when they did not start too well, there was always the argument that you couldn't freeze one, anyway.

This fierce pride felt by the owners of Franklins was almost as remarkable as the automobile itself. Long after the comaraderie of the road had become unsophisticated with other drivers, Franklin owners still went on blowing their horns whenever they passed each other. Very often they waved. By the same token, it would have been unthinkable for one Franklin owner to have passed another who appeared to be in trouble.

This was partly due to the Franklin-family feeling that the company fostered, as well as a natural curiosity to see who else had paid a couple of thousand dollars for an automobile.

Despite its price, (for those days) the Franklin was not a snobbish form of transportation. By and large, its owners fell into two groups: The completely unmechanical-minded, which included all women; and people like doctors who had to depend on their cars.

The riding qualities of the Franklin became a legend. Few people would dispute the fact that they were the easiest riding automobile on the road. Moreover, their reliability was something which made other car owners stand in awe. Unlike the Model T, almost no one except trained Franklin garagemen had much luck in repairing them. Therefore, most people left them alone. This may have accounted for their envious reputation.

Furthermore, the relationship between a Franklin dealer and the owner was akin to that of a doctor and a patient. In many instances, the dealer was a professional man who had fallen under the spell of the air-cooled motor and had forsaken his calling. The second Franklin that my family owned cost twenty-one hundred dollars, plus the pony. The dealer was a former veterinarian and dealt in horses on the side.

The Franklin flourished in an era when people took pride in being different. And there was little doubt that the air-cooled automobile gave them that privilege. Except for the last few models made in the early thirties, when the company was finally forced to bow to convention, Franklin styling was unique. Even its highly partisan owners were secretly aware that they were driving the homeliest car on the highways.

The sloping round hood that narrowed down to almost nothing at the front was the distinguishing feature. It was a result of realistic minds. Franklin engineers saw the problem for what it was. Having no radiator to contend with, they saw no reason for boxing in space. They didn't. Eventually, they got the hood down so close to the engine that its paint blistered from the heat.

To correct this they raised the hood around 1925 to a new and equally remarkable design. Unfortunately, however, it was about this time that degeneration began to set in at the factory. They tried to make the Franklin look like a car. The engineers put a lion on the snoot to make it resemble a radiator cap. From then on, the car was doomed.

In its heyday, though, the Franklin automobile was tops. It was not as radically different as the Stanley Steamer, but it was enough to satisfy most individualists. Each car had its own peculiar whirring sound caused by the big air fan. The gear

shift worked exactly the opposite way to any other car except
the Dodge.

The Franklin did have one disadvantage which owners
only mentioned in whispers. That was the problem of bugs.
On a summer's night these could seriously annoy a Franklin
automobile. The fan drew air down through a series of fins on
the cylinders. When the moths and bugs were out in force,
they plugged up these fins and caused the engine to overheat.
It was not unusual on a warm evening to see a Franklin engine
running merrily after the ignition had been switched off. This
was believable to any owner because even under the best of
conditions their engines sometimes got hot enough to fire
the gasoline without a spark.

Probably the most curious feature of the car was its
wooden frame. They said that it made them ride easier. It also
caused a unique sort of automotive trouble. They were subject to dry rot. When that happened, owners called in a
carpenter. He simply chiseled out the infected part and spliced
in a piece of ash.

On the other hand, some of the engineering features of
the Franklin look good even today. It had a special sort of
starter that operated on a twelve-volt battery. After the engine
started, this turned into a generator. For that reason no one
could stall a Franklin. Below a certain speed the starting
mechanism went to work again. Women especially loved this
feature. In traffic, a good many of them simply chugged along
on their starters.

And finally, the Franklin had one peculiarity that set it
apart from all others. The horn button was on the door, and
you blew it with your knee.

Both the Model T and the Franklin, as well as dozens of
other makes, were responsible for a unique sort of institution

that became known as the country garage. In the grand old days of motoring, these were a good deal more than simple purveyors of gasoline and oil. Very often they served as the nerve centers for a multitude of activities, including the exchange of second-hand cars, repeating shotguns, and deer rifles.

Knight's garage fell into that category by virtue of a reputation established in 1910 that it could repair anything propelled by petroleum or gunpowder. In addition, its founder, the late Fred Knight, garnered a certain amount of local fame as a friend of college presidents, a counselor of the young, and as a philosopher with a niche in history slightly above that of Socrates.

In time, these admirable traits were transmitted to his son, Harold, who has since added luster to the family reputation. This reached a high point of some sort the week before Christmas some years ago. Harold suddenly decided that it was time the garage stood treat to its numerous customers who had made the year a prosperous one. So on the afternoon of the twenty-fourth, the energetic proprietor started making preparations. Foremost of these, of course, was the purchase of egg-nog, punch, and other sinews of Yuletide cheer. When this was accomplished, however, the next problem was finding a place to serve the refreshments. The logical choice seemed to be the big flat-top desk in the office adjoining the garage.

This decision represented more than a mere expedient. It was symbolic of an era. During the lifetime of the desk, more pairs of feet had probably been placed upon it, and more good talk had been spoken across it than any similar piece of furniture in the state of New Hampshire.

To get down to its oil-stained top, however, was something else again. Upon it rested the accumulation of thirty-six years of automotive history. But young Knight was persistent. He removed the twenty-seven old sparkplugs and the four dead coils and placed them carefully on a shelf. He took the two dry-cell batteries that had come out of a telephone box when the company switched over from the crank system in 1924 and put them on the floor.

Next, he picked up the pinion gear that went on Mr. Adams' car that was out in the garage and put it in a drawer where he could find it the following day. Then he took the three shotgun shells and stuffed them in his pocket, and he threw the water pump from an outboard motor into a corner.

By this time, he could actually see parts of the desk, so he knew he was getting somewhere. He meticulously stacked up various pieces of reading material that among other things illustrated the differential mechanism of a 1916 Reo truck. There was a momentary problem of what to do with the Model T steering wheel, but he solved that by hanging it on a spike. By now, whole sections of the desk were visible.

The remainder of the materials considered necessary for the proper operation of a country garage—the ignition points from a Stutz Bearcat, three radio tubes, a nail file, two paper cups, seventy-six nuts and bolts, and a stuffed owl—he swept into a large cardboard box to be replaced on the morrow. With that accomplished, he was prepared to meet his guests.

Well, the word spread around town pretty quickly that the refreshments were on the garage, so to speak, and it wasn't long before cars were lined up at the gasoline pumps to a considerable depth. There were five or six professors from the State University, a dean or two, and a dozen instructors, as well as twenty or thirty townspeople. There was also old Jake Edgerly who wore his bearskin coat and managed to hit the spittoon pretty regularly, considering the amount of refreshments that he was inhaling. In addition, there were sundry others who discovered suddenly that they had motor trouble and needed to drop in at the garage.

Naturally, the host didn't have too much time to tend to his business, so he put a mathematics professor out on the gasoline pumps, and this fellow did fine except that he couldn't make change very well. In one corner of the office, an electrical engineer sat down with his egg-nog and took apart the generator that went on Ollie Johnson's truck and fixed it so Ollie had to buy a new one the following week.

After everybody had imbibed the spirits of Christmas for a while, things began to get pretty lively around that old desk. They sang a few carols that sent Harold's dog baying out into the woods, but then somebody started telling stories about motoring in the old days. Presently a suggestion was made that there ought to be a prize given that afternoon for the tallest tale that anybody could recall about driving an automobile. Right off, the proprietor set the three shotgun shells out on the desk among the bottles and told them to go ahead.

Lots of old-timers told some whoppers about the Model T's, but it was left to Jake Edgerly to go off with the shells. After everybody had had his say, Jake shuffled forward, opened his bearskin coat, and commenced to talk.

"You folks," he said, "may not recall that I had the first flivver in town. That was along about 1912, and the roads w'unt very good, but I started in doin' a jitney business to and fro from the depot." He shifted his cud to the other cheek. "Well, one afternoon," he went on, "this feller from Philadelphia gets off the train and says that he is thinkin' about buyin' a piece of land up here in the country. He wants to know if I can show him some of them abandoned farms. So I says, 'Yeah, if you don't mind riding in a flivver.' He says he don't, so off we goes.

"We got through town all right and was just startin' down the old church hill when I leaned back on the steerin' wheel so as to get a good purchase on the pedals, and I'll be jiggered if that gosh-danged wheel didn't come right off in my hands. There was nothin' to steer by, and that flivver goin' lickety-split out through the brush and over a stone wall and down toward the mill pond. My feet was all mixed up in the pedals, and I was yellin' 'Whoa!' like merry blazes.

"Well, sir," Jake went on, "presently we fetched up among the alders along the pond with our front wheels in the water. By this time, I was shakin' all over and wipin' the sweat off my forehead, and here's this city feller settin' there as cool as a cucumber. I'm about to say somethin' when he looks at me and then at the steering wheel, and then he says calmly, 'Mite loose, ain't it, Jake?' "

THE THEORY and practice of heating our houses in New Hampshire during the winter months have occupied the attention of the inhabitants since about 1623.

Out of this vast experience there have evolved two distinct schools of thought. On the one hand, there are those who believe that it can be done; on the other, there are the realists who know that it cannot.

Somewhere in between these two uncompromising attitudes lies the truth, and that is what we intend to explore here. In the course of this fact-finding, we shall probe the subjects of storm windows (pro and con), the modern furnace (friend or foe), the old-fashioned fireplace (help or hindrance), and of course, frozen water pipes (or setting fire to the house with a blow torch).

But first, let's make no mistake about it. New Hampshire gets cold in the winter. It is warmer than Antarctica, but averages about the same as the North Pole. Along toward the last week in January, our thermometers go haywire.

A neighbor of mine once called a friend of his who lived farther down the Point one frosty morning to brag

When Winter Comes

that his thermometer was registering forty-five degrees below zero.

"Good heavens," the voice answered on the other end of the line, "that isn't very cold. Down here the mercury has dropped three clapboards below the bottom of the glass."

Anyway, it gets pretty cold sometimes in these parts, and even more frigid in the mountains, but the truth is that thousands of us survive each winter, and that is what keeps the race going.

Shankhassick is fairly typical of the colonial type farm house, built on the top of a windy hill in 1685, and now converted into what the advertisements would call a "charming old place," complete with a snug den in the former woodshed. The paneling is magnificent, but the temperature of the floors registers a consistent fifty degrees from November 1 through April 15.

This is caused by four or five defects peculiar to old houses. The foundations are not tight. There is no cellar under the structure. The doors are fitted closely enough to keep out cats, but not mice. And the windows rattle a good quarter of an inch each way. This last is the result of generation after generation of aggravated menfolk complying with requests from nagging wives to "do something about that window that sticks." Short tempers and sharp planes have taken their toll, and the only remedy is to install storm windows.

This seems to be true of all of our old "gems" here in New Hampshire. The old-fashioned double-hung window with the little thumb catch on the side is an institution all by itself. Only those people who have grown up alongside of them, or whose forebears did, can satisfactorily master the technique of operating this type of opening.

Take an average but intelligent person, say with an I.Q.

of 180, and confront him with a double-hung window having a little catch, and he goes to pieces. This is because the thing is too simple for twentieth-century minds. Moreover, the windows were not designed in the first place to be opened. And, if anybody did succeed in getting them up, they were planned to stick on the way down. No other window could make that claim.

To one familiar with them, however, they present no real problem. The most workable technique is to approach them with an attitude of friendliness and trust, and a few Band-Aids. Press the little catch with the right thumb. Then give the sash an exploratory push with the left palm. If this fails to jar it loose, hit the window with considerable force. Then apply the Band-Aids and fetch the wrecking bar. For the first twenty years of my life I took this in stride, not knowing that somewhere, some place, there were windows that went up and down easily.

Except for this slight hazard, though, no one can deny that the colonial house was well built. They had to be, or they would not have lasted this long. Their builders seldom used paper under the clapboards, so the house's natural tendency was to let the wind go through instead of tacking around it. However, the old-timers knew a thing or two about insulation, just the same. Corn husks were sometimes used to fill the walls. Rats and squirrels helped with the job. Brick partitions were often built inside the walls on the north side.

By now, though, most of the real "gems" in New Hampshire have been converted to oil furnaces. At Shankhassick we went them one better by installing two of the monsters. One happily gulps oil to warm the northwest end of the house, while the other purrs contentedly in the southeast corner. When both of them are turned on full blast, fluctuations are noticed in petroleum stocks on Wall Street.

However, with these two oil-mad machines, on a real winter's day, with the temperature at twenty-degrees below zero and the wind coming out of the west at thirty-five miles per hour, we pretty much confine our activities to those rooms in which water does not freeze. On those days my wife transfers the butter from the cupboard to the refrigerator to keep it soft.

However, in spite of the fact that oil is making inroads on the heating problem of New Hampshire, it has not completely taken over. There are still thousands of homes that are heated by wood alone. Their occupants appear to be just as healthy as we more effete neighbors, and they are certainly wealthier. But the amount of wood that they use is something to conjure with. I have thoroughly explored this situation, and I am prepared to state that the old quotation of cutting your own wood and you warm yourself twice is about as erroneous as anything ever said.

As a matter of fact, wood cutting warms you eight or ten times. Once when you fell it. Again when you stack it. The third time when you haul it in from the woods. Four more times when you saw it into shorter lengths. Again when you pile it on the porch. And, finally when your wife tries to tell you how to get a good blaze going.

When I moved back to the old place, I had some hazy dreams of long, cozy winter evenings, curled up in front of a roaring fire with *Moby Dick* before my glazed eyes, listening to the wind howl outside. I soon found out differently. By some odd quirk of mind, the furnace men located the thermostat hard by the fireplace. When the flames began giving out heat, the thermostat shut off, and the rest of the house dropped to the freezing point. So, I gave up that dream and now plan to finish *Moby Dick* over the course of the next ten summers.

But because most of the early fireplaces have no dampers, it is touch and go whether they are profitable to use anyway. Many of us make a practice of stuffing newspapers into the chimney to cut off the draft. But, once removed, they cannot be replaced until the following morning. This is roughly comparable to leaving a window open in the living room with a huge fan blowing in cold air. One mason declared that dampers could be installed in our chimneys satisfactorily, but that was two years ago, and I have about given up hope.

Another New Hampshire winter rite that probably frightens insurance men into traumas was, and still is, the use of the common blow torch to thaw out frozen pipes. It is safe to say that few New Hampshire colonial home owners get through a winter without resorting to this trick. Curiously, no pipes in the Granite State ever freeze. They catch. They catch in the kitchen and in the back bathroom. Surprisingly, too, they never seem to catch much. Thus, a true native says, "Yes, it was pretty cold last night. My pipes under the kitchen caught a little."

Well, once they have caught a little, there are two or

three possibilities. One is to wait until spring for them to thaw out. Another is to move to Florida. But, the most effective, and the one that is preferred by people who like to live dangerously, is the use of the fine, old-fashioned blow torch. If it does not set fire to something in the starting process, it most assuredly will later.

Those of us who are experienced grasp the flaming instrument and crawl in under the kitchen, putting out the small fires as we go. We then locate the offending pipe by noting where the beams have been charred before and apply the torch to it. All of this requires the use of gasoline in a confined space, and it is quite exhilarating.

To forestall the problem of catching, many of us used to set lanterns close by the pipes during the evening. It was the final chore before going to bed. Nowadays, we run an electric cord in and leave a bulb burning. It takes very little extra heat to keep water pipes from freezing. But that is the whole nub of the problem here, anyway. If we could just get a little more heat to the proper places, our troubles would be over.

None of this is intended to alarm prospective purchasers of old New Hampshire "gems." Of course not. Right at this moment I am working in a comfortable sixty-five degrees at the ceiling and a healthy fifty degrees on the floor. By using special typewriting mittens, I can make the old machine fairly hum. Moreover, the coolness is partly caused by a hole in the wall where the old gutter drain went through the house and into the cistern. By actual count, twenty-seven workmen slaved on this building at various times, but they never managed to plug up that hole. Now, by the time anybody gets around to it in the spring, a couple of wrens have moved in, and they rent all summer.

On old houses, a good deal can be accomplished by storm

windows and insulation. There are two kinds of the former. There is the aluminum job that fits tightly, keeps out cold air, and can almost, but not quite, by pushed up and down by a woman. However, it tends to offend the true exponent of colonial architecture. For these people there is the time-honored storm sash with the wooden frame and the multiple panes.

The process of taking these off and putting them on is almost as exciting as playing with the blow torch. The supreme moment comes when the ladder rung breaks and the whole mess—homeowner, ladder, and storm window—goes crashing to the ground below. It is quite a sight.

In New Hampshire, Nature has thought of everything. From December through March, because of the state's high latitude, the sun never climbs more than a few degrees above the horizon; and then it is only seen on alternate Thursdays. We consider this a definite advantage. Otherwise, the continuous shining of the sun on the white landscape would cause wholesale snow blindness.

Moreover, Nature has even thought of the dangers of stagnant air. That is why she keeps that northwest breeze blowing throughout the winter at an average twenty-three miles per hour.

By February, the whirring of the oil burners can probably be heard on the moon. The only louder sound in our winter air is that made by the citizens themselves. This is variously described as the chest cough, the hacking cough, the smoker's cough, and pneumonia. If wet feet do not get us, the snow shovels will. This in turn is an advantage. It keeps the medical profession on its toes and ready for the skiing season.

New Hampshire is noted for this exciting winter sport. Public and private interests have spent huge sums to contrive a method for carrying middle-aged men to the top of a mountain by means of lifts, and then bringing them down on toboggans. Medically, the results are known variously as fractures, sprains, wrenches (as in a wrenched back), and a sort of catch-all term for dislocations. I have often thought that it could safely be said that New Hampshire and Vermont have revived the sport of tobogganing.

On those rare occasions when I go outside of the Granite State, I seem to meet with a good deal of misinformation concerning the suspected isolation brought on by our northern winters. Lamentably, this is not the case anymore. For some obscure reason, the cooling air, the falling snow, and the shivering body bring out the organizational instinct in men and women here.

After December 1, large members of the population spend their evenings enmeshed in parliamentary procedures. Primarily, these are concerned with installing new members and discussing the $87.23 that constitutes the treasury.

For winter in New Hampshire is the time of the club, the organization, the auxiliary, and the association. Because of the confining aspects of our cold months, people tend to huddle together in too-warm halls and listen to secretaries' reports.

Once in a spirit of pure research I confronted the people of Durham with a typewritten list of the organizations that flourished here. It required one whole, single-spaced sheet of typewriting paper. Admittedly, this is a college town and the seat of the State University. Apparently it is called the seat because that is where so many people sit on winter evenings, getting talked at. But the point was that no well-adjusted person ever need sit at home for a single evening all winter.

My listing excluded the dozens of bridge clubs, some of which play with anywhere from forty-eight to fifty-two cards, the morning coffees, the ever-present cocktail parties, and the discussion groups that discuss the other groups.

Here and there throughout the village, as well as in the rest of the state, somebody may be forced to remain at home for a winter's evening, but that is his own choice. Isolation is dead. The era of the president, the secretary, and the treasurer has taken over.

However, there is one bright spot. In any population of six hundred thousand there are bound to be a few mavericks. Persons, for example, who do not want to go to the Men's Club to hear about South Asia, or life in a fishing village, or dime store science. (All scheduled one season in Durham.)

For these people, the winter holds untold pleasures. To begin with, there is reading. There are days in the woods, cutting brush. There are deer hunting, smelt fishing, and conversation helped along with a southern product made from corn. Not the jibberish of cocktail parties, but good solid talk about transmissions, beavers, the old days, and boats. There is also that strange invention that brings horses right into your own living room.

For still others there is snow shoeing through silent woods with steaks burned over open fires. And, last but not least, there is snow shoveling. This is truly the universal winter sport in New Hampshire. When Old Man Winter descends on the Granite State, he spreads his blessings impartially.

The technique of dealing with it is simple. Grasp the shovel firmly and throw the snow over the left shoulder. Continue thus to the garage.

By March, this sport has become old hat, but then Nature thinks up something new for our entertainment. This is an impressive atmospheric disturbance that brings on sleet. Sleet is rain that falls on objects, generally electric power lines, when their temperature is below the freezing point. By natural processes, the rain forms ice, and the ice breaks the lines. Technically, this is known as a power failure. But it is far more than that.

It is a clarion call to the pioneer instinct that lies dormant in all of us. As the lights go out, the water supply fails, the furnace dies, and the electric stoves quit, a true New Hampshireman's pulse beats faster. He comes face to face with nature in the raw. Even his electric blanket no longer works. He looks reality squarely in the eye.

Then, like his forebears, he brings in wood, cooks over an open fire, scorches the paint, and drips candle wax throughout the house. But, for a few hours at least, he starts to live again. Then, just as he is getting ready to go out with his gun and come back with meat slung over his shoulder, the power company truck arrives, and he reverts to paying his electric bill and fetching food from the freezer. Unfortunately, New Hampshire can only produce a couple of these happy interludes per winter.

Even in this latitude, a warming trend has to come sooner or later. By March the snow shovel has lost its charm, and the oil bills have become a calamity. That's when our winter should quit and go away. But it seldom does. It roars through March and out again. It produces snow in April. Then comes the one week of spring, and suddenly it is summer.

The scenery becomes monotonously green. The shovels and snow tires are put away. The frozen plumbing is replaced. The challenge has gone.

But we real natives of the state do not remain disheartened very long. We know that these unpleasant conditions cannot last much beyond Labor Day. By that time, our oil burners will have started up again, our snow tires will be on, the shovel located, and our treasurer's report for the first meeting of the season prepared.

And then, dead ahead, lies the hunting season.

WHETHER they know it or not, all the wild creatures in New Hampshire belong to the state. The fact that some of them dwell on your land is no reason why you should consider them to be your animals. According to law, anybody can walk onto your property, blaze away with a howitzer, slay his game, and depart unmolested.

The cost of killing a man outright, through accident, has been established by custom as five hundred dollars and loss of hunting license. This last is considered very serious.

These rather arbitrary views on the part of the state make for a good deal of friction between landowners and hunters. Each fall, a certain number of cows get shot, a few hunters are felled, and the so-called deer-kill is about equal to that of the population.

For a long time, the director of the Fish and Game Department has valiantly tried to defend the right of hunters to cut fences, shoot out windows, block driveways, and pepper our houses with birdshot. He and the state trace this natural right back to the first settlers who were tired of being put in prison for poaching on the King's land. They did not actually describe the new

Great Hunting Episodes

right in the state constitution, but they got some laws passed on it in a hurry. Since then, the animals have had the dubious advantage of belonging to everybody.

I hunt. I like hunting. I go gunnin'. But I like baiting the Fish and Game Department even more. Each fall, I limber up the typewriter, point it toward Concord, and blaze away at this antiquated statute that compels us landowners to walk warily in our own woods from October through December. But I am grateful that fish and game personnel read the stuff. I have heard that they refer to me as "that newspaper fellow down in Durham." A kind of agitator, really.

The first year after I returned to Shankhassick, two hunters, exercising their rights, started a deer in a field near the house. Dawn was just coming up behind them, and without bothering to figure the trajectory of their opening barrage, they placed the first bullet just to the right of the shutter in the upstairs bedroom. The next round thumped harmlessly into an elm tree by the porch, and the final slug whistled over the top of the ridge pole.

In the meantime, the doe beat it for the river and swam out of sight. This was harmless enough, though very poor shooting. But the racket woke me up, and I got to thinking about deer hunting in fairly broad terms. For five hundred dollars, I could shoot back, but that didn't seem worth the expense.

Or I could start taking pot shots at the hunting fraternity through the newspaper. I figured that if anybody really sat down and considered the whole subject objectively, he would most likely throw his gun away and take up bowling. The type of rifle being used by a majority of the hunters at that time were more powerful than those carried by the Japanese Army during the war. Not only were the bullets larger, but they were propelled faster and farther.

Yet for a few dollars, anybody could buy a license and begin spraying lead about the countryside, regardless of whether he was color blind, feeble-minded, or incapable of holding a gun steady. Furthermore, the state encouraged this madness. Its publicity boasted through advertisements in metropolitan newspapers that hundreds of thousands of deer and people in New Hampshire could hardly wait each fall until the shooting started.

So I hopped out of bed and wrote a column concerning these misgivings and sent it off to Manchester.

When this appeared in the Sunday paper, I almost immediately noticed a chill in my relationship with local fish and game club members. I slugged on, however, with a feature story which included an interview with the real director of fish and game for the state.

In this, he assured me, as well as other landowners, that the careless spraying of lead about the countryside was actually the work of only three percent of the licensed hunters in New Hampshire. This was good news, but I accompanied my story with pictures of a large bullet hole in my mail box, hunters sitting under No Hunting signs, and a posed photograph of a hunter stalking a pheasant under my kitchen window.

The paper duly printed the story and distributed it to what we like to think of as our hundred thousand readers. The reaction was mixed. To some, I had been too gentle with the deerslayers. I was obviously in the employ of the Fish and Game Department. To others, I was a misguided ogre who was trying to stamp out the last form of amusement and recreation available to he-men.

Nevertheless, the piece did bring in a batch of interesting stories about hunting that more or less proved that New Hampshire was ripe for a change in its thinking about indiscriminate hunting on private property.

A horse had been mistaken for a moose and killed in the western part of the state. A Jersey heifer had been brought down and actually lugged off to Massachusetts under the impression that it was a deer. A neighbor told of finding a hunter's car blocking his driveway one Sunday morning, so he locked all the doors, and threw the key into a pond nearby. Another was sitting on his porch when high-powered shells began whining around his head. Tracing the source, he discovered that two hunters had set a target high up in a tree and were firing at it with bullets that carried over two miles.

A housewife reported that a hunter had chased a pheasant across her lawn and finally bagged it under her front steps. Still another told of five hunters passing around a bottle at seven o'clock in the morning outside her house and then blasting away at the insulators on the power lines.

All of this added up to an enraged citizenry, and the following year at the Durham town meeting the voters passed a local ordinance which made it illegal to hunt on a person's property without his written permission. This action was duly reported in the press, and the hunters of New Hampshire turned purple. The Fish and Game Department took it to court, and in due time established that a town could not interfere with the rights of an animal to get shot in any municipality in which he chose.

However, the purpose of the ordinance had been served. The word got around that on Durham Point, landowners looked with disfavor on flying lead every fall. Since then, most of the shooting has been our own.

At this point, my relations with the Fish and Game Department were somewhat less than cordial. The local warden did not drop in as often as he had before. On these previous visits, I had been a great fellow, having written a highly complimentary piece about him for the state magazine. That was when I learned that the Fish and Game Department had more officers with the power of arrest than our highly efficient State Police. However, I didn't mention this oddity in the story. It somehow made things look as though New Hampshire thought more of its animals than it did of its people.

But then, quite unexpectedly, I became a wonderful guy again, at least to one division of the Fish and Game Department. For several weeks that fall, members of this division called regularly twice a week, and we sat in the living room and talked about animals for a couple of hours each time. It was a highly enjoyable affair, and I think we all learned a good deal. They received the benefit of my views about Massachusetts hunters, and I garnered reams of information about deer. It was odd how it came about.

As I have already admitted, I like to hunt. On fall afternoons when the air is brisk I take the shotgun and start around my hunting trail. This is a path which I have cleared that leads first to the cabin by the river, then along its bank for a ways, cuts over a hill, and comes out in a grove of pine near the barn.

Partridges and pheasants are fairly numerous here. They seem to like the path, too. Except for one mistake a couple of years ago, I have never been able to inflict any damage on them. They seem to know the exact moment when I am tying my shoelace or lighting a cigarette, or have forgotten to push the safety catch. They take off with a mighty beating of wings, and I swing the gun up about the time that they are coming down a quarter of a mile away. It is harmless fun for both of us, and except for the pheasant which almost flew into the barrel of the gun one time, I have not decimated the bird population very much.

On one of these afternoon swings a couple of years ago, I was sneaking craftily along my path when I heard a twig snap. Thinking that perhaps the birds had decided to take the gun away from me, I turned around to look.

It was not the birds which were creeping up on me, but two deer. They were browsing on the bushes as they ambled along, and after they had spied me, one of them trotted up quite amiably and licked the barrel of the gun which I was holding in my arm. Then she lapped my hand a couple of times and walked off into the woods. I watched them for another ten minutes before they crossed into a field and disappeared.

I could hardly wait to get home and prepare a column for the Sunday paper, describing to my erstwhile friends in the Fish and Game Department the skill and cunning required to kill a deer. I made a good thing out of it, what with the does stalking me and lapping my hand and the shotgun, and I preparing to defend myself against attack. I wound it up with some fairly heavy-handed observations on our intrepid hunters who through skill, knowledge of the woods, and sub-machine guns, were able to search out and bring down an animal about the size of a St. Bernard.

The piece did nothing to cement relations with the nim-rods of the state, but at noon on Sunday my telephone rang, and a woman's voice said, "I think I have the answer, Paine. Those were two tame deer which we have been using for nutri-tion experiments at the State University. They got out of their pen about a week ago. I'll be down this afternoon, and we'll trap them."

Helenette Silver, a research worker for the Fish and Game, arrived presently and described the deer. The one that had lapped my hand did have a scar on her right ear. The other was less friendly. This fitted what I had observed earlier in the week, so we took a swing around the path.

We did not locate them that afternoon, but on the fol-lowing day, they turned up in the front field. Mrs. Silver had said that these deer liked tobacco and apples, so I picked up a couple of filter-tips, the kind that "tastes good like a cigarette should," and approached them slowly. The same deer walked up to me, sampled the tobacco, and then went on with her browsing.

I reported this to Mrs. Silver, and the next afternoon she drove down from Concord with a deer trap. This was a pen with a door which banged shut when the deer put her weight on the bottom board. We baited it with apples and several kinds of cigarettes in case the deer were smoking more but enjoying it less, and then adjourned to the house.

With the deer season scheduled to open in two weeks, Mrs. Silver was anxious to trap the deer before some bold hunter brought them down by hitting them on the head with a stick.

During these very pleasant sessions, while we waited for the two deer to stumble into the trap, Mrs. Silver told me some hair-raising stories about hunters who had tried to poach other tame deer kept by the Fish and Game Department. Then we examined minutely a specie known as the Sunday hunter, and after we had worked that one over, she departed.

By now, several members of the Fish and Game Department were involved. It was fairly ludicrous. One afternoon, a station wagon arrived with pellets for the deer. Then a truck turned up with another trap. The telephone wires hummed between Durham and Concord whenever the deer were sighted. In a week's time, the state was expected to resound with the thunder of guns, as several thousand hunters invaded the countryside in search of deer. Yet, here we were, trying to save two does.

On a state-wide basis, I did not retract my piece about deer hunting and its glories, or that the does had been tame, but I did spread the word locally. Mrs. Silver came down twice a week until the season opened, but the deer were never around when she was here.

The first day of the season, a hunter got "his" deer farther down the Point. Then on the second day, late in the afternoon, I heard cannonading to the south. There were twelve shots in all, and after that the two deer were never seen again. The next day, a neighbor was boasting at the garage that he had got one deer and his son had got the other. Mrs. Silver came down and examined the photographs of the historic sporting event, and identified the deer as the tame variety.

However, there was one mystery that she and I were never able to clear up. How could anybody have used twelve shots to bring down two pet deer? Were they fired in self defense? We never did find the answer to that question.

The reaction to all this was interesting. The distinction that people made between killing tame and wild deer was marked. In fact, this generated so much ire that within a week every piece of land for a stretch of four miles had been posted against hunting. And the rogue, or perhaps innocent perpetrator of the deed, had been universally condemned by his neighbors. Occasionally, nowadays, I hear him firing listlessly at clay pigeons, but he has never really gone into the woods to hunt again.

One of the curious aspects of game in the Granite State is that while the partridges, pheasants, quail, and deer belong to the people of New Hampshire, the ducks and geese that choose to fly over us belong to the federal government. They require a different license, and they have their own wardens.

Apparently thousands of federal employees are working tirelessly to save the ducks, but from what I have seen of duck hunting along my river and bay, Uncle Sam should think more about protecting the hunters who pay taxes and support the government.

At one time, I thought it would be a great thing to get up in the dark, stumble down to the river, and shoot ducks from a dinghy. Other men did, and they seemed to enjoy it. They bragged of freezers filled with buffleheads, golden eyes, mallards, geese and blacks. And for each duck there was a different theory about how to cook him. The amount of time spent discussing this improbability along the New Hampshire seacoast accounts for about one week per year per inhabitant.

The wild duck, when properly cooked, is a tasty dish

and has become a great favorite with many of the country's leading gourmets, including starving cats, men who have been lost in the woods for three weeks, and families which are reduced to eating their snowshoe thongs.

After procuring the duck, either by scaring it to death with shotgun blasts or waiting until one drops dead of old age in the air, you must remove the feathers. This is preferably done in the kitchen or living room where it adds zest to the marriage relationship.

As hunters know, nature has endowed the wild duck with a protective covering which is twice the thickness of the bird itself. The experienced gourmet begins the plucking process without glasses. After a while he puts on his reading specs. Finally, when most of the feathers have been removed, he calls for a magnifying glass. This is so that he can see the duck that is now emerging from beneath the feathers. The whole process requires less than an hour.

The bird is then cleaned and prepared for the oven. Over the years, a good many different schools of thought have evolved concerning this vital step. One group believes that peanut butter is essential to the proper cooking of these delicate game birds. According to this school, the duck is boiled and the meat removed. But instead of throwing this away, they cover it over in a baking dish with approximately seven pounds of peanut butter. The various sections of the duck are then lost in the resulting mass, and most people think they are simply eating baked peanut butter.

The turnip school, on the other hand, favors the use of that obnoxious vegetable to disguise the taste of the duck. They rely principally on the theory that the real gourmet will eat the turnip in preference to the duck and go away happy. Furthermore they believe that somehow the turnip absorbs the taste of the duck through a chemical process understood only by men who have worked years in the laboratory. As yet, however, no one has offered definite proof that the turnip doesn't feel as badly about the whole thing as the prospective diner, or the duck.

Still a third group of realists feels that the onion should play an important role in the preparation of a wild duck. They base their philosophy on the fact that a good, healthy onion can disguise the flavor of almost anything. Therefore, they boil the duck with onions. They stuff it with onions. They bake it in a sea of onions. The duck emerges unscathed from the oven.

Others advocate apples, fruit juice, cranberries, and old oranges. These are piled in and around and under the duck. They are then discarded, and the duck is brought to the table. There are those who believe the process should be reversed.

The cooking time of wild duck varies from twenty minutes to three hours. However, it apparently makes very little difference how long the duck is cooked. One safe rule to follow is that the longer the bird is cooked the more likelihood there is that it will catch fire and perish mercifully.

Our most successful New Hampshire chefs combine the best points of the several schools. First they parboil the ducks. Then they smother them in peanut butter, turnips, fruit juice, onions, apples, cranberries, and old oranges. After that, they bake them for three hours, and broil them over an open fire for thirty minutes. At this point, the true gourmet drops them slyly into the flames and invites his guest to go out for dinner, or simply to eat the plates.

Somehow, my few ventures into the duck world, either as a hunter or as a diner, were never very enjoyable. I always came off second best to the ducks. The one time I tried to serve buffleheads to guests I pulled a shoulder muscle carving the birds and was laid up for two weeks.

As for capturing the ducks, few people will admit that this sport is really yachting under extremely unpleasant conditions. In New Hampshire, most of the shooting is done from small boats which leak. Getting down the river to the Bay is actually cruising in the dark on a very cold morning. And sitting under a frosty tarpaulin in an inch of salt water is excruciating.

Combine these hazards with wet gloves, a gasoline drip from the outboard motor which discourages smoking, and a wrenched back caused by slipping down the ramp to the dock prior to the start of the voyage, and you have a pretty general idea of duck hunting.

When dawn finally comes, the normal heartbeat of the hunter had dropped to about twenty-five per minute, his body temperature registers seventy degrees in the shade, and a northwest wind has sprung up and caused the anchor to drag. While he is fixing this, the prey suddenly come winging out of the east, warm and rested after a good night's sleep, and moving through the air at forty miles per hour. The chances are excellent that they will be flying over Providence, Rhode Island, before a New Hampshire hunter gets his gun from under the tarpaulin, removes his gloves, and takes aim. If a duck is unlikely enough to fly directly into the boat, he may get hurt. Otherwise, the odds are on his side.

Then, regardless of how the great hunt turns out, there is always that long voyage home. Spray hurtles over the boat. The outboard runs out of fuel. Both oarlocks have been used as anchors for the decoys. Detaching these with half-frozen fingers, and fumbling with a knife that won't open, while drifting rapidly toward the middle of the Bay, is only one aspect of this fine recreation.

There is also the homecoming. For some reason, known only to a wife, the sight of a would-be duck hunter staggering up from the river, his back bent low from lying in an eight-foot dinghy for three hours, invites derision.

"Well," she jeers, "look who's here. The hunter home from the hill. Where are the ducks? Where's the meat? It must have been a massacre."

In cases like this, about all the hunter can do is wonder to himself whether duck hunting really comes under the definition of a sport. Self-imposed torture is probably a better term.

GEORGE WOODBURY, author of *John Goffe's Mill* and *The Story of a Stanley Steamer*, lives just to the right and slightly below me on the editorial pages of the Sunday paper. His weekly "Home Town Histories" and his book review section are as well read as anything in the sheet. For a while he tried his hand at various newspaper tasks, and one of my pleasant assignments when he first joined the staff of the paper was to take him with me one day to demonstrate how I gathered material for a feature story.

As I recall, we had been sent out to do a piece on the growth of some small town close to the Massachusetts border. We spent the day interviewing the town clerk, the local librarian, some real estate men, the school principal, the police chief, and the one man we found in the street.

Then we adjourned to a diner and discussed his Stanley Steamer. After a while, he returned to Manchester, and I drove home to Durham. But that day marked a turning point in both our careers. As far as I know, he had been cured of any desire to write feature stories, and I had been introduced to the subject of antique automobiles.

The Antique Car Restorer

My life has not been the same since. Sparked by George's contagious enthusiasm, I straight-away embarked on the restoration of the old family Franklin that had been purchased in 1917, and had lain dormant in the barn since 1931.

In a previous chapter I have attempted to describe the esteem with which the Franklin was regarded in those early days of motoring. It was not as highly individualistic as the Stanley Steamer, but it was air-cooled and it was superbly built. Moreover, it was constructed almost entirely of aluminum.

From 1917 until 1924, my particular Franklin had been the Paine Family's principal means of transportation from Durham Point to the village and the neighboring city of Dover. Daily, it had plowed through mud, snow, heat, and dust to take us to school, get the mail and paper, haul home provisions, and carry the family to social affairs at the Grange Hall.

When it was new, my sister and her bridegroom, a young second lieutenant about to leave for France, had driven the car through the White Mountains on their honeymoon.

In 1925, when my father bought another Franklin, he decided to trade in the pony instead of the old car. You could do this in those days. After that, the two cars were referred to as the old Franklin and the new Franklin. The fact that the old one outlasted the new one was due to a couple of fortuitous circumstances.

In 1931, a front wheel came off in the driveway, and the old car was pushed into the barn for the last time and retired. During World War II, the scrap drive spurned it because the body was made of aluminum. These two things, plus our family trait of preserving junk, accounted for the old Franklin's being there the afternoon that I returned from talking with George Woodbury about antique automobiles.

My brother and I had already embarked on the restoration of the house and barn, so the Franklin was pushed to the new garage. The wheel that had come off in 1931 was still held on by a nail through the cotter pin hole. The wooden frame on the port side had rotted out some time around 1926 and sagged a good deal, but otherwise than that the whole thing was intact. The side curtains, though considerably chewed up by nesting squirrels, were complete, and a search of the barn eventually turned up the cover to the top.

The body styling was exactly the same as some of the most expensive convertibles made in America today. In front, there were two bucket seats, covered with black leather. Behind these was the rear seat that accommodated three people. It was a two-door model, and the significant difference from present day cars was that a person could climb into the back seat without banging his head on the top, or dislocating his back bone. The trunk was of course, smaller than today's models, and the rear tire rode upright on a holder just abaft of it.

Originally, the car had been painted a dark green, but

various do-it-yourself paint jobs had reduced this to a dull brown. The high windshield had been the victim of a baseball some time around 1928. When it became the old Franklin in 1925, certain liberties were taken with it in the matter of driving through brush and across fields. As a result, the front mudguards resembled lace work.

Thus, at the beginning there were three major repair jobs to be done. The first was installing two new frames, which meant taking the entire car apart, replacing the rotten wood, and reassembling the parts again. The next most important task was tidying up the lacy mudguards, and the third operation was the overhaul of the air-cooled, six cylinder engine.

I said then that it could all be done in six months. That was four years ago, but at the time I had not yet encountered New Hampshire auto body concerns or automobile mechanics. I was ignorant of the fact that the restorer of an antique car is looked upon as the comic relief in the everyday drudgery of garage work.

Things started off bravely enough. I took the mudguards to a blacksmith and metal worker in Dover whom I had known for many years. As usual we observed the formalities by not mentioning the contemplated job for thirty minutes.

"How have you been, Phil?" he asked.

"Fine," I said. "And yourself?"

"Oh, pretty good. Can't complain. A little arthritis. Also have been having some trouble with my stomach."

"Sorry to hear that, Bob," I said. "Do you think you would be interested in fixing up these . . . ?"

"Feet don't feel so good either."

I said that I was even sorrier to hear that, and then we went on to talk about superacidity, a submarine skipper who was a mutual friend, and the problem of trapping some squirrels that were nesting in an old washing machine on the second floor of the blacksmith shop.

Eventually, however, we did get around to the mudguards, and he declared enthusiastically that the best known welder of aluminum in the Northeast would be called in to do the job, and I could pick them up in two weeks.

In two months' time I went back and found they lying exactly as I had left them in the corner. Bob and I again discussed submarines, squirrels, superacidity, and arthritis before we got around to the mudguards. The welder had failed to show up, but that was because he drank. In New Hampshire, this term explains everything. The proprietor and I shook our heads sadly at this tragic disclosure, even as we prepared to depart for our own bottles, but he assured me that he would do the job himself. Except for a slight heart ailment that had been added to his superacidity and his arthritic condition, he was the second-best welder of aluminum in the Granite State.

In the meantime, I had completely taken the old car apart, removed the engine, and stacked the remains around the sides of the garage. George Woodbury had been methodical in the dissection of his Stanley Steamer. He had labeled his nuts and bolts, tagged the more obscure parts, and had maintained a place for everything. His training as an anthropologist, no doubt, accounted for this intelligent approach.

I tried to follow in his footsteps, but right off the system went wrong. The bolts to the differential tipped over and got mixed up with the nuts that held the body together; and then the floorboard screws got dumped into the box that contained cotter pins and engine mount bolts. After a while, it seemed easier to lump everything together and trust to memory. That, of course, was foolhardy.

The next thing to depart was the engine. A local garage manager, apparently acting on impulse, offered to overhaul it for me. He said that he would put his best mechanics to work on it when business was slack. And he did, too. Within a week, the engine had been taken apart, the various organs distributed in boxes throughout the garage, and the cylinders sent to a Portsmouth machine shop for surgery. This had something to do with the valves.

The status quo was now maintained for exactly two years. Then, at the beginning of the twenty-fifth month, the engine base was moved in the garage from the general area of the grease pit to a home closer to the furnace. At the Portsmouth machine shop, the cylinders had taken up lodging under a bench and seemed content to remain there. For some obscure reason, the proprietor defended his slowness by declaring that he had been looking for suitable valves in Georgia and Florida. To me, after two years in the strange world of automobile mechanics, that seemed probable.

About this time, I went back to see the second-best welder of aluminum in the Northeast. Again we covered the submarines, his arthritis, his heart condition, and in a general way, superacidity. My mudguards had weathered two winters comfortably in the corner, and I was glad to note that they had not deteriorated. Owing to various vicissitudes, he had not been able to "get to them yet."

However, he was prepared to forego this lucrative job, in view of the need for speed, and recommended the third best welder of aluminum in the Northeast. This gentleman operated a body works only a few blocks away, so we put the mudguards into the car and sped off. Bob acted as a kind of ambassador extraordinary, and after a while we were able to make contact with the owner of the body works, though it required most of a morning.

Once we had penetrated the outer defenses and actually stood in the presence of this important man, our reception was almost royal.

"Ah, Mr. Paine. Delighted. Read about the old car in the Sunday paper. Sure, we can fix you up. Make new ones, if you want. Okay, I understand. You want to keep them authentic. In that case, we'll fix these up for you. Like new. Come back in two weeks."

We put the mudguards in the furnace room between the oil tank and the hot-water heater. At least they would be warm and comfortable there, and not lying around under some cold bench. Then I thanked my ambassador for his courteous attention to the matter, left him some Tums, and returned home.

Although I made regularly monthly pilgrimages to that furnace room for a year thereafter, I was never able to see the great man again. Each time, however, I was grateful to note that the mudguards had not been mistakenly put on a 1955 Buick. They were untouched and as good as ever.

By this time, I had located some oak planks in Rochester, called in a boat builder by the name of Ned McIntosh to cut out new frames, and had reestablished the body in its proper place. Various parts were now scattered over two states, three counties, and four towns or cities. The Portsmouth machine shop had not come up with any good solution to the valve problem, even in Georgia, so it seemed time to start gathering the stuff together again.

I made three trips to Portsmouth just to retrieve the cylinders, and two more to look for the timing chain. I never did find this. Then I paid him forty dollars, presumably for storage, and bade him goodbye. My first inclination had been

to comment sharply on his mentality, his probable ante-
cedents, and his future prospects in the hereafter. But I didn't.
Instead I adopted an attitude of cold, silent rage. But I don't
think he even noticed.

At the local garage, they had made some progress by col-
lecting the various boxes of parts and placing them on a shelf
some twenty feet above a rack of old tires. The engine base,
however, remained near the furnace and had almost disappeared under an inch of dust.

Three years had now passed in the restoration of the old
Franklin, and they had been fruitful ones in my own garage.
All the paint had been removed from the body. The running
gear had been cleaned and painted. The brakes had been re-
lined. The several objects which had rolled out through a hole
at the base of the garage wall had been recovered and attached
to something. The boat builder had constructed a new battery
box. Even the fine old leather seats had been washed and
rubbed with polish.

The stage was now set for the big scene. This took place
at the local garage one warm summer evening. Heretofore, I
had played along as the comic in the affair, receiving their ex-
cuses graciously, and half admitting their contention that the
repair of modern cars was more important than restoring a
vehicle that obviously was not going to be used for daily transportation.

On this particular evening, I did not adopt the cold,
aloof approach. I backed my station wagon as close to the
engine base as I could, declaring meanwhile to the mechanic
whom I had known for years, that any interference would
bring the law down on his head, the manager's head, and the
garage owner's head.

The mechanic tried to reason with me, but I would have

none of it.

"Look, Steve," I said. "That's my engine. If I leave it here long enough for this garage to fix, the metal will disintegrate. It will get lost under the dust and won't be found until 1990. By the time this junkyard gets around to putting it back together, we'll be old men in wheelchairs."

Steve suggested that he ought to telephone the garage manager and inform him of this development.

I shook my head. "If anybody tries to stop me from taking my engine home tonight," I shouted, "I'll get the State Police, the local police, and the National Guard." This last was made as a threat. No one can call out the National Guard except the Governor.

Steve took this impassively and started to remove the boxes from the top shelf. Then he paused a moment and asked, "What about the sheriff, Phil? Did you forget him?"

This took some of the wind out of my sails, but not all of it.

"And another thing, Steve," I shouted, "you can tell your boss that I'll never bring a car in here again or pay him another cent as long as I live."

"You betcha," said Steve.

When we had collected the cylinders, the engine base, the three boxes of bolts and nuts, the distributor, the flywheel, and the crank, I made some more threats about the economic future of that particular garage and departed. I felt good. It had required three exasperating years to get angry enough to express my views on old car restoration and the working mechanic, but when the explosion finally came, it had been a satisfactory one. It had not impressed Steve, but that was because he had been my chief source of animal stories for several years.

That night, I slept better than I had for months. I went to bed visualizing the garage manager out of work and hungry, his children in rags, and his wife sick, all because he had stalled me off for three years on repairing the Franklin engine. To punish him further, I resolved never to speak to him again, and never to pay him for taking the engine apart.

The next morning the phone rang fairly early, and I answered. The voice at the other end was that of the garage manager, and he did not seem surprised at the previous evening's developments.

"Those new piston rings came in yesterday," he said. "You can have them if you want, or I can send them back."

I said that I would take them, and then I added that I was sorry the way things had turned out. He replied that he was, too.

I still hoped that the garage would fall upon evil days and "fail up," as we say in New Hampshire, but I had abandoned my desire to see his family suffer.

This was just as well, because by mid-morning I had discovered that the station wagon would not run, and by eleven o'clock the garage's big, red wrecker was in the yard. In the afternoon, the tractor broke down, and I had to ask the manager to send out a mechanic. Within three days, the threat "or pay him another cent as long as I live" had run into a bill of fifty dollars.

However, all of this had served as a definite step in the right direction. The status quo had been upset. The various parts of the venerable old car were coming home. Not repaired, but at least they were under one roof again. I retrieved the mudguards by simply walking into the familiar furnace room in Dover and hurling them into the back of the station wagon.

After three years of trying to deal with the automobile industry, I was still baffled by its reluctance to repair old cars. As far as I could tell, the money which the garages and body works would have received for the various jobs was of the same par value as money spent on more recent models. Yet, they never could seem to get around to fixing anything.

Interested, yes. Any part of the old car aroused admiration, curiosity, and enthusiasm when it was first taken to a garage. The promises were reassuring, but then nothing happened. Other restorers of antique automobiles reported similar experiences.

Soon after the engine and the mudguards had come back from their long vacations, I discovered the Hopey brothers. One of them lived in Madbury, and the other in Newmarket. From the very first, it was apparent that they had not learned the code about old car restorers. Instead of regarding me as a comedian, they treated me as a guy with a mechanical problem.

The brother in Madbury repaired my generator and my distributor in less than a week. He rewired the engine, and restored the old coil. The other Hopey received the mudguards without hilarity, promised to have them straightened out in four weeks, and did. Then he accepted the rear mudguards, fixed them up, put on a new tail light, and called me up when they were done.

Spurred on by this astonishing development in the automotive field, I put back the old valves, installed new piston rings, bolted on the starter, and placed the engine back in the car where it belonged. I bolted on the repaired mudguards. Then I went to see the Hopeys again. Would the one who lived in Madbury rewire the machine for me? He said he would, and did. Then I went to the other brother and asked him if he would paint the body green and the mudguards black. He said he would, but hasn't. However, this is because his regular customers have taken up his time. That excuse has a familiar ring to it and seems to spring from the automotive industry's instinctive distrust of money spent on old cars.

People have asked me if I would ever consider restoring another antique. I generally reply that one restoration is enough for any one man. To take a car, even an old one, completely apart and then put it together again is a fascinating pastime. Moreover, the mileage that a journalist can get out of the process is remarkable. Every so often I report to my column readers on the Franklin's progress. As a result, a good many of them have turned up here at Shankhassick to view the wreck. We take our stance with one foot on the running board, lean on the doors, and then just plain talk old cars until far into the night.

Two enthusiasts who remained until one o'clock in the morning actually came up with some good advice recently. "If you wish to continue to live happily with your present wife," they said, "don't ever let her know how much it costs to restore an old car. Wives just naturally don't understand about such things."

They apparently spoke from experience.

AFTER a Sunday column about my family's horse, old Charley, had been picked up by *The Reader's Digest* and reprinted into eight languages, my stature as a journalist grew by leaps and bounds.

A man in a state liquor store began shaking hands with me. My mother-in-law stopped trying to filch a copy of the paper from a trash barrel on Monday mornings and went out and bought her own, and a student of journalism at the State University came to see me one afternoon to find out how it was done.

I replied that the job of writing at home was an easy one, provided the writer thoroughly understood the basic problem of the telephone. I warned him that thousands of youthful Hemingways, tired stock brokers, plumbers, advertising copy writers, and waitresses were likewise planning to retreat to Maine, New Hampshire, or Vermont in order to compose literature in a quiet den beside a crackling fire—and that he had better learn the fundamentals early.

I explained that there was no such thing as a house without a telephone in the United States, and that he would have to master the technique

A
Columnist's
Life

of dealing with the instrument early in his writing career. I then gave him the benefit of my experience, which I am happy to pass along to others.

In the first place, the typewriter should be placed about twenty-three feet away from the nearest telephone, so that incoming calls may be heard clearly and distinctly. Otherwise, you will spend a good deal of time trying to understand what is being said.

For example, if the phone is at a greater distance from your writing area, you will only hear such provocative parts of your wife's conversations as "You're kidding?" and "Really?" and "When did this all happen?" Each time, you will have to stop typing in order to listen to what is being said. This cuts into your writing time, and literature is the loser.

With the telephone within twenty-three feet, however, you hear the whole conversation, decide immediately which of your wife's clubs she is talking about, and return happily to work. In this case, literature is the winner.

On the other hand, households containing two telephones present more of a problem. Suppose, for instance, that the instrument which is twenty-three feet away rings several times and then stops. The first question is: Has your wife answered the phone that is one floor and forty-seven feet away? Or, has the caller hung up?

In the event that the second possibility has occurred, you will have to stop writing long enough to ponder who it might have been, and whether the caller was phoning with information other than your wife's club affairs.

Did the call perhaps concern the broken lawnmower, the boat engine, the new trailer tire, or the deep well pump? Was it perhaps somebody trying to leave you a million dollars? Exploring these various possibilities takes time away from the old keyboard and can be costly. A quicker solution to the question of whether the phone has been answered downstairs is to shout, "Telephone!" at the first sound of the bell. This alerts everybody within a radius of two hundred feet that a crisis has come up, and somebody had better do something about it. It likewise informs the family that your responsibility in the matter has been terminated. Your writing continues on, and literature wins some more.

The likelihood of a writer's having three telephones is so remote that no young man need to concern himself with the third instrument. The important thing for youthful Hemingways, tired stock brokers, plumbers, advertising copy writers, and waitresses to remember is that one telephone should never be more than about twenty-three feet away from the typewriter.

Whether the young journalism student took any of this to heart, I never found out. He went away looking a little perplexed and somewhat suspicious that I had been pulling his leg. But I could not have been more serious. Either you understand the telephone or you don't.

Since that time, I have written approximately six hundred "Reports from the Village." Close to six hundred thousand people have admitted that they could have done them better. I hasten to agree with them. But if you break away from a salaried job in the city, you have got to be able to turn a hand to almost anything in New Hampshire. Moreover, a weekly column in a state-wide paper gives you a splendid opportunity to strike a blow for the things you do or do not believe in.

I happen to believe in machinery that runs. I like lighting fixtures that don't disintegrate after three weeks of use. I have never understood cake sales. Why don't the ladies all chip in a dollar for the cause instead of baking mediocre cakes and then buying them from each other?

All of these subjects are grist to a columnist's mill. The ordinary run of news during the past decade has been pretty dreary. Fires, earthquakes, small wars, threats from Russia, and automobile accidents have monopolized the headlines. The only light-hearted stories have come from the politicians in Washington and Concord, New Hampshire.

I have never been sure what my editor had in mind when he waved a couple of cigarettes in the air during our first interview and declared expansively, "Probe the local scene, Paine. Six hundred words, double spaced. Get them in every Friday."

About six years after that, and some three hundred columns later, we had another long chat about my work. "Look," he said, "the city room is complaining about your copy. For the love of God, can't you remember to leave a little space at the bottom of the page so that the city editor can paste the three sheets together? What? Well, for one thing, it wastes paste. Okay, okay, save your humor for the column."

Except for a few instances like this, the editor has left me pretty much alone. He called me a "mundivagant seer" once in print, but a professor at the State University explained to me that these were not cusswords, so I didn't sue.

You can have a lot of fun with a column in a small state. You get read by the Governor, your mother-in-law, your grammar school classmates, and employees of the state liquor store. Almost everywhere you go, somebody says, "Read your column last week. Weren't you feeling well?" Occasionally, a reader will miss the point. Then I feel embarrassed for both of us. One time I wrote a piece called "A Scientific Business Barometer" which spoofed the weighty methods of determining the state of the economy by college professors.

It was based on my own experience as a father of a young lady, aged ten, who one summer decided to go into the lemonade business on the front lawn. She printed her sign "Lemonaid . . . 5 centes," and her mother prepared the merchandise. I bought the first glass, and then a couple of soft-hearted neighbors strolled over, complaining of terrible thirsts. But after that, business fell off perceptibly, and from my den window I could see that American enterprise was entering a crisis. So I went out and drank a couple of more glasses of the bitter stuff.

That evening, after the firm had been saved, and my daughter was airily predicting a prosperous future for the whole family, I formulated Paine's Law of Superacidity. This was a lot of nonsense about determining the state of the economy by the number of anti-acid pills that a father was required to swallow in order to counteract the home-made lemonade that he had been forced to drink the previous afternoon. The better he felt, the better the shape of the general economy.

I dispatched this bit of foolishness to the paper, but the surprise did not come until a few days later when a woman asked incredulously, "You don't really believe that system works, do you? I mean about the lemonade and stuff."

This was such a shock that I replied as seriously as I could that of course it worked. The economic law was infallible. Moreover, I said, my own experience of the previous Sunday indicated that the time was propitious for purchasing stocks. In particular, I recommended the pharmaceuticals.

The woman was properly mystified and went away shaking her head. Oddly enough, I had bought some drug stock that week and it subsequently did go up fifteen points. But it is not a system that I would recommend for everybody.

In order to keep a column going for twelve years, a journalist has to invent certain methods of probing what the editor had called the "local scene." Almost everything about American television, radio, movies, scalps that breathe, wave sets that think for themselves, cosmetics, advertising, and electrical appliances can and should be spoofed. The sad thing is that more of it is not done.

One of the easiest methods is the fake interview. Here, as in the case of the woman and the lemonade, newspaper writing requires a clear labeling of fact and fancy. For one thing, the laws of libel rule out spoofing such comic figures as governors, representatives, senators, and presidential candidates. You cannot make them say things that they have not actually said.

But if you take a little man from Mars, for example, you can make him ask some pertinent questions, and then throw back the answers. Bring him down to earth and let him cast a fresh eye at American advertising's preoccupation with perspiration, for example, and you help your reader to see how dreadful the whole, sorry television mess is. Combine this with a standard Western show and you have got something that should make Americans blush, but doesn't.

The only drawback to columns of this kind is that readers begin asking, "Don't you like anything? Are you mad at everybody?"

The answer, of course, is that a "think piece," for example, on lemonade and the economy would leave the Sunday reader snoring in his rocking chair. After all, the subject is not too consequential. But to the man in the state liquor store, it was highly interesting. We shook hands enthusiastically the next time I went in, and after slamming a bottle good-naturedly on the counter, he asked, "How's the economy doing,

Phil? Is it going up or down?"

Another type of column that appealed to certain readers was the tongue-in-cheek report of a local event. A considerable amount of straight news radiated from the State University through a regular press bureau. But New Hampshire is so small that nearly everyone from the Canadian border to the Atlantic has some connection with the college, either as an alumnus or as the parent of a student, or a brother or sister of one. Thus, any news about Durham finds an audience throughout the state.

The time the bear came to Durham was certainly news, but it was hardly an item for the University press bureau. As I recall, the story got started one morning when a large black animal was sighted along the Boston & Maine Railroad tracks by a maintenance crew which was heading south on a hand car.

Bright and early the following day, a huge, black beast was observed ambling down the driveway of a local selectman. This was allegedly witnessed by seven residents who drew up beside the road and watched its progress.

This set the telephone system in motion, and by noon of that day it was common knowledge that a stampede of gigantic black bears had broken out of the north woods and was invading the village.

After carefully listening to accounts and cross-checking dozens of persons' stories who had not seen the bear but knew somebody who had, it was possible to arrive at the truth of this local sensation.

The train workers along the tracks saw either one bear, a mother bear and cub, or three snarling, vicious killers of the north.

The number of persons who were eye-witnesses to the

marauding black devil which was proceeding down the selectman's driveway varied from two to seven. The time of their
observations was placed at various periods between five in the
morning and 7 p.m.

The location of this driveway was pinned down to an
area covering roughly ten square miles. At one stage, the
number of driveways down which the ferocious animal had
ambled reached a high of seven. These included all three
selectmen, and four more residents whose driveways sloped.

The savage inhabitant of the wild was variously described
as huge, medium sized, no larger than a dog, and a tiny cub.
The one thing on which all the telephone newscasters agreed
was that what-ever-it-was ambled. It did not run, jump, slide,
lope, scurry, or walk. It ambled.

The animal's diet was likewise narrowed down to small
children, berries, honey bees, and garbage cans. Its over-all
dimensions when made into a bear rug varied from "covering
the floor of an entire room" to something about the size of a
small table top. On this subject, opinion was evenly divided
between those who thought a bear-skin rug would be just the
thing for a den and those who declared that it would only serve
to trip people up in the middle of the night.

To obtain this prize, and thereby secure the peace and
safety of the village, it was reliably reported that a posse had
gone forth with guns to slay the beast. It was just as reliably
reported that one man had started following its trail but had
given up.

All of this called for an investigation by persons interested
in tracking bears. There appeared to be quite a few woodsmen
who knew a bear track when they saw one, and the great
what-ever-it-was was followed over concrete, macadam, pine
needles, and lawns. The signs were unmistakable. A b'ar had

been there, along with several dozen close relatives.

On the other hand, there were skeptics. Spoil-sports, if you will. They pointed out that the village contained a large black dog. It ambled. It had long hair. It roamed. In fact, it looked like what most people believe a bear looks like.

But whoever heard of a plain black dog that could cause two hundred and thirty-four telephones to ring, absorb the attention of the village woodsmen for three days, and become the principal subject of conversation at four bridge clubs, eighteen social gatherings, and one hundred and seven individual conversations along Main Street.

I still think it must have been a bear.

FOR SOME reason, the fact that a person conducts a column or writes at home sets him apart from the rest of the employables. To many, it appears highly unlikely that a writer is actually engaged in his trade when he says he is.

Far more probable, they suspect, the columnist is doing one of several things. He is either sleeping, taking narcotics, enjoying himself in unheard of revels, or simply staring at the wall.

Although there are scores of occupations that permit the breadwinner to accomplish his work within the confines of his house, the writer is singled out as the one who best defies the custom of going away to a job each morning.

On the other hand, the journalist who takes advantage of this misapprehension can do things that would put a more respectable citizen under medical care. I recall that at one period the column was coming along harder than usual. During previous weeks, I had covered such topics as lunatic skiers, skins that breathed, the perspiration menace, and women drivers. It was time now for a change of pace.

Why not, I thought, do something that would keep readers interested for two or three weeks? Build up suspense. And attempt something that I had wanted to prove for twenty years? Why not plunge into the woods of New Hampshire with only a jackknife, an axe, a sleeping bag, a fish line, and a gun, to see if modern man could survive in the unfriendly climate of a northern winter. By the term, woods of New Hampshire, I meant a log cabin on the banks of the Oyster River, some quarter of a mile from the house. It contained a fireplace and a stove and a couple of cots that had been thrown out of the barn.

I felt that the idea would certainly catch the interest of the state's sportsmen. After all, any hunter who gets lost in the forest overnight during the fall shooting season is certain to rate front page treatment in New Hampshire dailies.

Consequently, without really thinking the project through, I ripped off a column, outlining my plan and urging readers to follow my adventures in forthcoming issues of the Sunday paper. Fortunately, I made no exact promises as to specific dates or the length of time which this Granite State Thoreau was going to remain in the wilds, gnawing on roots and berries.

My wife took a good deal of interest in the program. When I pointed out that this was no laughing matter, and that there was little that I would not do to keep my readers happy, she guffawed and said, "You know darned well that this has nothing to do with the column. You're just having a recurrence of your trapper phase. Your name is Jacque LePierre and you are running a trap line up around Hudson Bay somewhere. You catch de silver fox, and by gar, in the spring you see de factor at Whale River, and then, by gar, you snow shoe three sleeps away and marry Marie. I used to read those stories, too."

Actually, she could not have been more wrong. I pointed out that I was not Jacque LePierre of Hudson Bay, the trapper. I was Henry Thoreau on the banks of Walden, with a few kernels of dried corn from the garden, a pencil, and some yellow paper. If I could actually prove that it was possible to live in a log cabin and scribble off lofty thoughts by the light of the fireplace and a couple of candles, I would have then demonstrated beyond question that most of the men of the world were wasting their time on commuter trains.

Unfortunately, the weather refused to cooperate. By the time another column was due, the temperature had dropped to a brisk zero degrees. This was accompanied by a refreshing wind from the North Pole.

But the show must go on. The column must be written. I bade a reluctant farewell to my electric blanket, sharpened the axe and got a bucksaw out of the garage. I donned all the warm clothes that I owned. The unreliable shotgun, the fish line and hooks were tucked into the sleeping bag. The few ounces of dried corn which were taken along to tide me over until I could find some roots and berries were stowed in a pocket. I was ready to plunge.

All through history, there have been journalists who risked their necks to get the "big story." War correspondents constantly expose themselves to danger. And if TV shows can be believed, most crimes are solved by intrepid newspapermen. But all of these were mere afternoon larks compared to spending a day and a night in a log cabin with only a pencil and a few sheets of yellow paper.

Through sound planning, I had delayed my plunge until after a hearty lunch at the house. Thus, I went forth into the wilderness warm and contented. But by late afternoon, when I had chopped and sawed wood for three hours and had carried it into the cabin to be stacked, I began to get hungry. I set my fish line through a hole in the ice. Then I took up the gun and set out in search of meat.

By sunset, with the temperature hustling down to the zero mark again, I was ready to admit that dinner apparently was going to consist of dried corn and lofty thoughts.

There were no fish in the river to be caught. Not a single animal wanted to be shot. If there were any berries about, they had long since fallen from the bushes. Because of the frozen ground, it was impossible to get at any roots, even if I had known what I was looking for. There was only the dried corn.

Before departing from the house, I had re-read Thoreau's description of dried corn and its preparation. In the quiet warmth of the living room, the whole thing had sounded delectable. Pound the corn into a meal, mix with salt and water, and then fry like a pancake.

Soon, I had huge fires going in both the stove and on the hearth. Only twenty-eight percent of the smoke went up the chimney at first, and I had to retreat out the door every ten minutes to clear my eyes. But it was pretty jolly, just the same. One lone American against the elements with nothing but his bare hands, a pencil, some yellow paper, and dried corn. Out of this experience, I would get two or three columns, perhaps an essay or two, and the satisfaction of knowing that modern man could live without thermostats, automatic chokes, and instant foods.

Alas, those were the last printable thoughts that I had for twelve hours. The fried corn was a spectacular failure. It loosened a filling and cracked a tooth. The temperature inside the cabin varied from five degrees above zero to one hundred and twenty degrees above. There seemed to be no way to maintain a constant warmth.

Although eighty-seven percent of the smoke eventually went up the chimneys, there was still enough left to make a candle invisible at ten feet. When it came time to sit down before the fire and transfer any original and inspiring thoughts to paper, I could not even see the yellow sheets. My right hand was immobile from the cold. Tears ran down my cheeks. My stomach felt as though a mink had crawled into it and caught his paw in a trap.

But for the benefit of journalism I stuck it out. It was impossible to sleep, of course. The moment that the fires burned low, the temperature sagged toward zero. When dawn finally came, I was no longer Thoreau, the philosopher of Walden. I was modern man again, stumbling up the road to the house in search of thermostats, oil furnaces, the hundred-watt bulb, and instant foods.

My wife greeted me at the door. She had been watching the road for some time.

"By gar, Jacque," she said. "You catch de silver fox? Yes? Now you go see Marie?" I intimated that this was not the time for jokes. So she grinned and said, "Okay, Thoreau, come

on in. There are bacon and eggs and coffee and frozen orange
juice in the kitchen. Then you can have a nice hot bath and a
shave and get under your electric blanket. I'll take the phone
off the hook." She paused at this point. "By the way," she
asked, "Did you learn anything?"

"Yep," I said without hesitation. "Thoreau was a liar."

Through persistence, I eventually got a couple of columns
out of that night in the cabin. But one was not at all what I
had expected to write. Instead, I pointed out what a marvelous
invention electricity was. For a few paltry dollars a month, it
comes humming over the lines and powers electric blankets,
oil furnaces, and garbage disposals. It cooks foods. It furnishes
light and entertainment, and it opens cans.

The other concerned cabin life in New Hampshire during January with particular reference to the density of wood
smoke required to blind a person permanently for life. The
fact that the whole thing had been a journalistic failure; and
that there were stories which could be better covered by a reporter in a warm room with the telephone ringing, were not
mentioned. I just let friends and readers continue to believe
that columnists have all the fun.

ONE OTHER hazard of the column business is the unselfish
desire of many readers to furnish ideas. Almost anybody can
think up better subjects than the columnist. In some cases,
these turn out to be life-savers. Others are pure propaganda
and are quickly recognized. For a good cause, though, most
columnists will say a few kind words.

Moreover, these suggestions often come from the most
unlikely sources. Only recently, I was nonchalantly plowing
my driveway when a police car roared to a stop beside the

tractor. I checked quickly to see if my number plate had fallen off. Then I watched while my State Police friend, Cliff Hildreth, heaved himself out of the cruiser and walked over to me.

"What is it, Cliff?" I said. "Are you going to make a pinch?" He looked pretty serious and business like.

"No, Phil," he said. "I was just wondering whether you ever used ideas for your column. I think I know a dandy."

I replied that I frequently did, especially when they came from the State Police.

"This is a good one," Cliff said. "There's this fellow up in my neighborhood that's got a crow gun. It works on bottled gas, and he sets it to start shooting at five o'clock. There's some sort of a timing device on it. In the spring, after he has planted his corn, that damned gun starts banging away every morning. Makes a hell of a noise. Wakes up the whole neighborhood. Somehow the gun injects a shot of bottled gas in the chamber, and then something fires it." Here he paused and chuckled. "Occasionally, three or four charges go into the chamber before it fires, and then it sounds like a Sherman tank having a tantrum. There's the devil to pay. Neighbors complaining. Dogs barking. Everybody threatening to sue." Apparently, just the thought of it made him feel good, for he put his foot on the tractor and laughed out loud. "And the comical part is there isn't a damned thing anybody can do about it. The guy is just scaring the crows out of his corn and earning his living."

I assured him that the story sounded like a dandy one, sure enough, and I would be up in the spring to interview the owner of the gun.

"When it first started banging," Cliff said, "I thought to myself, 'There's a column for Phil. He's always complaining about crows and raccoons in his garden.'" Then he looked over at the police cruiser. "My God," he said. "I almost forgot. I got to be going. There's been an accident down the road here."

A city journalist certainly reports more important news than his country cousin does, and he makes more money doing it, but I have often wondered whether he gets as much enjoyment out of his work. In my public relations days, a friend who worked in New York kept urging me to go to that city and get into the "big time."

The only answer I could think of to give him then was an incredulous, "Why?" That was several years ago, and he has not come up with a satisfactory reply yet. In fact, only recently he was inquiring about land in New Hampshire.

THE ATTITUDE of our Durham citizens toward their local government can be accurately judged by the length of the annual Town Meeting.

If the voters choose to authorize without quibbling a new fire engine, four street lights on Mill Road, a new culvert on the Point, and an air compressor for the department of public works, then the selectmen may be sure that satisfaction reigns among the citizenry.

Furthermore, the temper of the town can be sensed by the amount of light-hearted spoofing that accompanies these discussions. For example, at a Durham Town Meeting once, a local wag got to his feet after a prolonged argument about the fire hydrant situation and pointed out that the question of dog licenses was likewise involved. "Why," he asked, "should dogs in the outlying districts where the fire hydrants were few and far between pay the same amount for tags as those which dwelt in the center of the village? Was there not some relationship between the fees which dog owners were asked to pay and the number of available hydrants near them?" This observation got the meeting back on

The
Little
Republics

the right track, and the voters went on to the business of
street lights.

On the other hand, if the citizens haggle about the price
of a welding machine for the water department and question
the advisability of purchasing new hose for the fire engine,
then something is wrong. A meeting that is prolonged longer
than a morning session indicates that the tax payers are feeling
the pinch of their previous year's largess.

New Hampshire Town Meetings have been the subject
of journalistic probing for the past century. The towns themselves are called Little Republics, and the meetings are termed
"Democracy in Action." The journalists sit in the back row,
and the moderator sits up front. Not far away, the town clerk
stares out belligerently at the voters, daring them to question
his past year's figures. Usually, to the left, the three selectmen
lounge at a table, prepared to defend their honor to the last
man.

When things have been going right, and taxes have been
kept low, and the garbage is being removed regularly, and
the town dump has only caught on fire twice during the year,
they gaze happily at the ceiling.

But, woe betide the town officials if a bridge has collapsed
during the year, or a tree has been removed from Main Street,
or the sewer mains have been extended in the direction of the
town clerk's home, or a sidewalk has been built four inches
onto private land. Then the criticism becomes general and
extends to such momentous decisions as rubber boots for the
town crew.

The only real consistency in these New Hampshire meetings is the weather. During the second week of March, the
annual fracas is generally accompanied by hail, sleet, snow,
rain, wind, and before the discovery of macadam, by mud.

This combination of the least attractive of Granite State elements is known as "Town Meeting Weather." On occasions the heavens throw in a little lightning.

Here in Durham, the advancement of civilization has all but destroyed the basic character of the Town Meeting that existed until about twenty years ago. The meetings are now held in a University building, complete with air ducts, microphone, and steam heat. The articles are discussed in precise, professorial, Midwestern accents. Only a few forthright individuals from the outlying districts of the village have survived, and though they do the best they can, the original vigor of the meetings has been lost.

But thirty years ago, things were different. The annual get-together was held on the second floor of the old Town Hall. Heat was provided by a cast iron stove that glowed quietly in one corner. Huddled close to it were the Hollow Tree Folk. These were so named because it was generally believed that they inhabited such trees, coming out once a year to the Town Meeting, but then retreating to their lairs again. They were never seen at any other time.

There were about a dozen of them, some with mighty beards, all with bearskin coats, and their jaws worked methodically on pieces of tobacco. A good deal of the residue flowed onto their beards, but this in no way hampered their aim or their determination to hit the red hot stove lid that marked the bull's-eye.

It went like this. The moderator would drone, "Article five: To see if the voters will authorize the expenditure of three hundred and fifty dollars for the purpose of adding four new street lights to Madbury Road. Petitioned by Lucy Adams and ten other legal voters."

As he began reading, twelve jaws would stop moving.

When he had concluded, twelve jets of tobacco hissed on the stove simultaneously. Inasmuch as these gentlemen never spoke, it was hard to judge whether this indicated approval or disapproval. However, their accuracy did produce an aroma that wafted itself gradually over the hall like fog. This, combined with the pungent power of wet fur coats, culminated in a ripeness of atmosphere not unlike an Eskimo igloo.

In those days, the town warrant frequently contained choice items that an alert reporter would pick up and send to the wire services. On one memorable occasion in the Durham warrant an article proposed that the town authorize a sum of money to "pave the road from the doctor's house to the cemetery." It referred to a contemplated extension of a street which was best known by the fact that the only doctor lived on the corner. It terminated in an Indian burial ground. But the item was used by newspapers all over the country.

The following year, the cemetery committee, impressed by this unexpected notoriety, began its annual report with, "Things were sort of dead in the cemetery this year . . ." By that, they intended to convey the idea that only one lot had been sold during the previous twelve months. But, this kind of humor was a little too macabre for most editors to stomach.

As a rule, our Town Meetings tend to concentrate on four or five major issues. These include the town dump, trash removal, street lights, water and sewer, and the Memorial Day parade. For this occasion, most budgets contain an appropriation of one hundred dollars to pay homage to old soldiers. And although few people dare to question the righteousness of this expenditure, a majority usually express themselves as being in favor of hiring a better band than the one that furnished the music the previous May.

In the past few years many towns have appointed budget

committees to go over the proposed expenditures before the meetings. Working with them closely is the League of Women Voters which holds prevue meetings prior to the big day.

Curiously, the remarkable thing about these is that they in no way change anybody's viewpoint. Often an article that has been approved by the budget committee goes down before a hail of nays. Contrarily, the voters will increase the appropriation for something that catches their fancy. One year the need of rubber boots for the town crew was described so appealingly that the citizens approved enough money to buy rubber boots for the next twenty years. Just the storage problem became quite awesome.

In almost any New Hampshire town you will find one lone man who through his consistency, his out-spoken criticism, his bull-headedness, and his splendid opposition becomes known as the Great Opposer. He is against everything from the Memorial Day parade to the new arc welder. He opposes water, garbage, trash, sidewalks, education, roads, bridges, rubber boots, and the veterans' memorial. Moreover, he makes his stand clear on every issue. But he is allowed his say, and that marks the difference between local government and that circus in Washington. At a Town Meeting anybody can flay the hide off the authorities and know that he is reaching the intended victim. Who knows whether those telegrams ever really get to our senators in Washington?

It is these local authorities who are the unsung heroes of the Little Republics. They are the true defenders of Democracy, working for a pittance and being awakened twice a week at one o'clock to answer the eternal question. "There's a dead cat on Main Street. What shall I do?"

Let there be a discrepancy of six cents in the town's funds, and the citizens are out baying at their heels. Remove a tree from the center of town, and voters start holding meetings.

The remarkable thing about local government is that there always seem to be enough men willing to remove those dead cats from Main Street.

Looking to what is termed the state level of government, New Hampshire has in Concord, a Governor, a Governor's Council, a Senate, and the third largest legislative body in the world, known as the House of Representatives. Almost anybody in the state can "go to the legislature," if he is so minded. Because our population is so small, and our newspapers so alert, the state government offers little opportunity for graft. If there is corruption, it can only be found in the mileage allowances paid to our officials. For five or six legislators to form a car pool and ride in one car while individually charging each expense account with mileage is about tops in civic debauchery.

The Governor and Council may have some unseen functions that make them necessary, but their primary purpose is to amuse the citizens. During one particularly dull summer, they enlivened things for the whole newspaper-reading public during several months. Somehow or other, they got entangled in what became known as the Great Seat Controversy, and they held the public spellbound from early spring until October.

Primarily, the controversy came about as a result of the tender and solicitous attention which the State of New Hampshire was then devoting to the buttocks of its Representatives. Whether these stalwarts would be able to sit down on anything when they convened in January that year was viewed with mixed emotions by most voters.

On the one hand, the thought of our lawmakers returning to work and finding no seats in their illustrious hall had some elements of humor. This was tempered, however, by the realization that a standing politician automatically opens his mouth, as though his jaw were attached to his knee tendons. The possibility of four hundred politicians all spouting nonsense at the same time was a sobering influence.

The Seat Controversy served as a remarkable demonstration of the ineffectiveness of the Executive Council method of state government. Moreover, it proved beyond a doubt that five determined Councilmen can stymie the best intentions of any Governor, cost the state additional tax dollars, and get booted out of office for their pains. This did not go unnoticed by the citizens.

It came about this way.

The previous Legislature, noting with some dismay that the floor beneath it was rotting away, appropriated a sum of money to repair the underpinnings, paint the ceiling, and install new seats. Tacked onto an appropriation bill, it went merrily through the House and Senate and was signed by the business-minded Governor named Lane Dwinell. Thus it was law.

However, the joker was a harmless, little sentence that was marked with an asterisk at the bottom of this particular piece of legislation. It stated, "Provided that before any plans are adopted they must be approved by the Speaker of the House."

The Speaker was a respected politician from Stratham, and by all accounts an able man in the House of Representatives. According to reports, he wanted a type of seat similar to those in theaters . . . comfortable, strongly made, and durable. His own particular desire was that the seat itself fold up completely against the back so that late-arriving Representatives could squeeze by their fellow lawmakers.

Like most state projects, L'Affaire Chairs was turned over to the Public Works Commissioner. Still innocent of the dynamite that was contained in this seemingly harmless pastime, he put the seats out for bid.

Two firms, the American Seating Company and the Mainco Trading Company, submitted bids in due time. They proved to be slightly over twenty thousand dollars, but Mainco's bid was about two thousand dollars less.

In the meantime, the two companies had demonstrated their chairs in the Council chamber, and it was the consensus of the Commissioner of Public Works, the Governor, and House Speaker Scammon that the American Seating Company's product was the better one for New Hampshire buttocks. Consequently, after they had all tried out both chairs to their complete satisfaction, the Commissioner recommended that the Governor accept the higher bid. The idea of the Governor and the Speaker of the House jouncing up and down in those chairs during working hours left the voters pretty impressed. No detail of state government was too trivial to be overlooked by the Chief Executive.

In making his recommendation, the Commissioner of Public Works pointed out that the American Seating Company's chairs came the closest to meeting the specifications, though they did not meet them completely. The Mainco chairs, on the other hand, differed from the plans in fourteen particulars. This, in the opinion of the Governor, the Commissioner, and House Speaker Scammon, was enough to justify the higher price of the American Seating seats.

But it did not impress the Councilors. Under the New Hampshire form of state government the Governor's Council can stymie the Governor whenever it wants to by refusing to approve his actions. On their side, they cited the fact that

Mainco chairs were distributed by a Granite State firm. Thus they played on the natural instincts of New Hampshire people to buy at home. They promptly refused to approve the purchase of the American Seating chairs.

Instead, they instructed the Commissioner to put out a request for new bids. This time the Council told him to get five bids. Unfortunately, there were apparently only two companies in the area who cared whether the New Hampshire Legislature sat down or not. Presently the same two firms came back with new bids. They were both slightly higher than before.

Stymied.

The Council refused to approve the Governor's recommendation, and the Governor was not backing down on his Commissioner of Public Works or his Speaker of the House.

Then the Council had a bright idea. It would call in the Speaker for a conference. He was asked to liberalize the specifications. He tightened them. The Speaker did agree, however, to insert the words "or equal" into his plans. This was supposed to get around some small technical differences between what he wanted and what the New Hampshire distributor was offering.

So once again the long-suffering Commissioner of Public Works put the seats out for bid again. The results were similar. By this time the weekly Council meetings were being watched with growing enthusiasm by the voters.

The fact that a member of the House of Representatives was also a representative of the Mainco company, as well as chairman of a county committee for an aspiring Republican nominee for Governor, served to cloud the issue. It was, however, publicly acknowledged that his commission on the Mainco chairs would have been about two thousand dollars.

By this time it was no secret around the State House that the Department of Public Works had spent a good deal more than the difference between the two bids in officials' time and paper work. This was reported to be almost five thousand dollars.

In the meantime, a special session of the Legislature had been called to deal with a tax situation. At the end of this, most of the lawmakers returned home bearing their old seats with them. This solved the disposal problem, cheered the weary legislators, and added urgency to the need for new seating facilities.

The Councilors, however, were still unimpressed. Statesmen all, they now decided to try a new tack. They waited until the Governor had left for Europe on a vacation. Then they tried to ram the Mainco chairs past the Acting Governor. But the latter was loyal to his chief.

By now the public was ecstatic. Things were getting livelier. The Attorney General then entered the act. He told the Council bluntly that even if the low bid was accepted he would order the State Treasurer not to pay the bill on the grounds that the Mainco chairs were "not responsive" to the specifications. That meant that they did not meet the plans or requirements.

This should have given the Councilors pause, but it did not. They seemed intent on proving the claim that they were the most stubborn and obstinate public officials in New Hampshire's long history. They went to work on the Acting Governor again. But he would have none of it.

The first sign of a break came in October. The intriguing circus was drawing to a close. Enter now a Manchester businessman, one Joseph H. Geisal, and a member of the House of Representatives. At the age of eighty-seven, he was in no mood to stand up during the forthcoming session of the Legislature. He walked into the State House one day and disposed of a problem in five minutes that a newspaper declared, ". . . has had the Governor and Council stymied for eight months."

What he did could only have happened in a small state. He gave his personal check for $23,143.80 to the Attorney General, which was the exact price of the four hundred and six American Seating Company chairs. He said something about its being a "disgrace." He also made it plain that this was a private transaction between himself and the American Seating Company, thus requiring no Council approval.

"I have full confidence," he added, "that the incoming administration, no matter who is Governor, and the members of the incoming House of Representatives will reimburse me. This is a matter of honor. They are not bound to reimburse me."

But of course they did, and everybody had one last good guffaw. The Commissioner of Public Works got the chairs installed in time for the next session, and the Governor returned rested from his European trip. As for the strong-minded Councilors, one did not seek renomination, another was renominated, and three were roundly defeated at the polls later on.

The Legislature could now be seated.

While all of this was taking place, New Hampshire's famous "eighth wonder of the world," the Old Man of the Mountain in Franconia Notch was having a far from dull summer. Not only did clouds of controversy swirl about his aging Profile, but the deeper furrows of his forehead became involved in an acrimonious debate that eventually drew in the harrassed Governor, state geologists, the Associated General

Contractors of New Hampshire, some of the state's news-papers, a Massachusetts weatherproofing firm, the state's Rec-reation Division, and a good many idle spectators.

The one clear fact that emerged from the furor was that the Old Man's forehead was indisputably slipping out over his nose, and unless this could be checked, the State of New Hampshire was going to have to replace this historic attraction with something less majestic.

The differences of opinion stemmed from several basic questions. Was the great stone face eventually doomed to go crashing down into Profile Lake at the foot of the mountain, regardless of what measures were taken to preserve it? More-over, had there been enough study of the problem? Was the Old Man a Democrat or a Republican? And, finally, was the state doing enough merely to pin his massive brow to the more solid granite where his brains presumably are?

Chronologically, the hassle started when the chief of the Recreation Division let loose with the opinion that the Great Stone Face was doomed to eventual extinction anyway. State engineers pointed out that, "The same forces that carved the face in Franconia Notch are now irresistibly at work to destroy it." This weighty opinion left most people cold, but it did prompt one paper to take up the matter of sonic booms caused by the "space-happy" Air Force, and Westover Field in Massa-chusetts caught a good deal of criticism. This was purely a side-light to the affair and the newspaper got right back to the main theme. Would the state accept a crusade on the part of the New Hampshire press to save the Old Man?

The Governor thought not. Nevertheless, he did send his Public Works engineers to the top of the mountain to inspect the Profile's forehead. At the same time, he turned down an offer made by the Associated General Contractors of New

Hampshire to conduct at their own expense ". . . a complete and comprehensive geological study of the Profile." This did not please anybody.

However, it did rouse up the sleeping politicians. Early in the game, the man who had finally solved the seat contro-

versy, Joseph H. Geisal of Manchester, stepped into the picture with the declaration that at the next session of the House he would introduce a bill to appropriate "one million dollars or as much as is necessary to preserve the Old Man of the Mountain as New Hampshire's greatest asset."

Later on, though, he hedged somewhat by declaring, "If

the good people of my ward return me to the next session, I will, etc., etc." By this time people were beginning to wonder whose side the Old Man was on. The Councilmen, although deeply involved in the seat controversy, liked what they saw. They jumped in with both feet and began estimating the stone face's value to be in the neighborhood of one billion dollars. Inasmuch as nobody could offer any better figures, these were accepted at par.

The Governor in the meantime was discovering that though the Old Man sat serenely up there above the clouds, apparently oblivious to things in Concord, he actually was at heart a master politician. The Chief Executive's first step was to become more cooperative with the press. Furthermore, the evidence for a comprehensive study of the situation was piling up.

The previous Legislature had appropriated twenty-five thousand dollars for the sole purpose of anchoring the Old Man's forehead more securely, and the Governor now proposed on the recommendation of his engineers, that a weatherproofing job be done on the sinister fissure that was developing just below the Profile's hairline.

The contract was let to a Massachusetts firm for about ten thousand dollars. At the same time, the Recreation Division warmed up and went to some pains to describe what was happening on the top of the mountain. It warned hikers to keep off the Old Man's head. The fissure that was causing the stone forehead to slip was forty-four feet long, a foot wide, and seven feet deep, No one cared to dispute this statement, not even the Manchester papers.

The Division also divulged that the contract with the weatherproofing firm called for installing a "pressure plug" at the bottom of the fissure with a quick-hardening agent to prevent leakage. Once that was done, the company planned to fill the crack with an especially concocted "intrusion grout" under twenty pounds pressure. By this time, the president of the weatherproofing firm wished that he had never heard of the Old Man of the Mountain. For days he had been under considerable editorial attack because his company was not the largest one of its kind in the world.

However, he kept his temper while siding with the anti-Governor forces on the matter of a geological survey. He even issued a public statement. "We cannot know exactly what we are doing because there is not a thorough or even adequate geological survey of the Profile. But we will do our best in a difficult situation." Whereupon, he and his crew disappeared up the mountain side.

Behind them they left a good many people who agreed wholeheartedly on the matter of proper surveys. Lined up solidly with him and opposed to the Governor were the Manchester papers, a large consulting firm in New York, the state geologist, and the operator of the largest granite quarry in Concord.

By now the politicians were beginning to look elsewhere, having discovered that they had a bear by the tail. The state geologist pointed out lugubriously that the weatherproofing job might hasten the collapse of the famous landmark. He went on to say that no geological survey had even been authorized by the state authorities. "I have not even been consulted in the matter," one paper quoted him as saying. "Not even on the specifications." He then went on to admit that he had spent one day four years before on the Old Man's forehead, but "most of the day was consumed getting up and down the mountain."

His warning about the possible collapse agreed with that

of the New York geology firm. The latter likewise advised the Governor that the weatherproofing job "might trigger a sizeable collapse." The Chief Executive chose to ignore this on the strength of a survey by his Public Works Department which assured him that no harm could result from the project. The engineers were photographed standing on the disputed slab of granite that formed the Old Man's brow. The picture received fairly wide distribution.

After the waterproofing party had vanished up the mountain side, trouble struck from another direction. A quarry owner, and therefore considered familiar with stone, blasted away, "Tar . . . not intrusion grout, is the only adequate and safe weatherproofing." This advice was ignored by all but the editorial writers.

In fact, none of this was being lost on the newspapers. The proffers of private help which they extended were in the best traditions of the state. The Manchester papers, possibly with an eye on circulation, again offered to conduct a campaign to collect money to restore the Profile. Eventually, however, this turned into a full-scale investigation on the part of the newspaper to determine whether the director of the Recreation Division had actually informed the Governor of this generous offer. Apparently there was some suspicion in the editorial chambers that the Governor did not read that particular paper.

Then after a month, while people waited to hear the mighty splash of the Old Man's forehead falling into Profile Lake at the base of the mountain, the Massachusetts waterproofing firm came down from the clouds and quietly returned to the Bay State. For the first time in nearly thirty days the Governor, the Recreation Division, and the engineers of the Public Works Department were able to breathe normally again. Their estimation of the corrective steps to be taken had been correct. Intrusion grout, not tar, had been just the right thing for the Old Man's forehead. Thus, another great crisis in New Hampshire politics was overcome.

T
HE PAST fifty years in Durham
have witnessed some astonishing
changes. The main street has been
paved. The student body at the State
University has grown from seven hundred to more than three thousand. The
town dump employs a full time watch-
man. School children ride to school
instead of walking.

Building permits are required by
a village ordinance for anything larger
than a box trap. The Hollow Tree Folk
have all but disappeared. Only the
river, the weather, and Shankhassick
have not shown any tendency to
change.

Noting this, a professor of history
at the University observed recently to
me, "You Paines," he said, "have roots.
So few families anymore have roots.
The children grow up on wonderful
old places like Shankhassick, but then
they move away to California and
Tulsa and Peoria. After a while, all
they have left are memories, and even
these tend to fade out. But not you
Paines. You've put your roots down
deep."

I assumed that he was referring to
the junk in the barn, and assured him
that we intended to hire a truck some
day and dispose of that problem.

"Now
Ve
Is de
Characters"

"No," he said. "I don't mean that. The junk is part of it, of course, but what I had in mind was your complete and unflagging enchantment with Shankhassick, Durham, and New Hampshire. That's a rare thing nowadays. There's a continuity to life on this old place that you don't see very often anymore."

I took this to be a compliment, but it was a thought to ponder just the same. Perhaps there was something good in being able to predict where each section of the stone walls was going to tumble down during the winter. Maybe knowing every tree, every gully, every square foot of field and woods on fifty acres was sort of unique in this era of mass migrations.

The professor may have had a point. So I told him how the roots got started.

Only a chance meeting, I said, between my father and a Yale classmate named Jim Sawyer at the Parker House in Boston during the spring of 1907 made us New Hampshire folk instead of Maine natives.

The story of that encounter probably got embellished in later years, but the way my mother used to tell it made us believe that some divine power had guided the family to New Hampshire and Shankhassick. As we heard the tale repeated during the next forty-five years, my father had taken a trip from New York, where he was working as a newspaper reporter, to Castine, Maine, in order to purchase a farm and write. The decision to get out of New York and try his hand at fiction had been made. The only thing that remained to be done was to locate the perfect country place and set up shop. At the time, he apparently was intent on beating that era's version of the "rat race."

According to the legend, he had arrived in Castine with a real estate advertisement in his pocket only to learn that the farm which he was interested in had been sold the previous day. Disappointed, he had returned to Boston and registered at the Parker House.

That evening, as he was going into the dining room, presumably to order the tripe, a voice exclaimed, "Why, Ralph Paine. What are you doing here?"

My father turned to see Jim Sawyer, who was then treasurer of Phillips Academy, Andover, rising from a table and coming toward him. As former inhabitants of Yale, they went through the usual warm greetings, and then my father explained what had brought him so far north of New York City.

"Jim," he said, "I've just lost a farm."

"Lost a farm," Sawyer exclaimed. "How could you lose a whole farm?"

My father told him about the real estate advertisement and the Castine fiasco, whereupon Jim Sawyer looked thoughtful for a moment, and then asked, "What sort of place are you looking for, Ralph?"

"Well," my father is alleged to have said, "In the first place, it has got to be on salt water."

"I see," said Mr. Sawyer.

"And it has got to have a colonial house with about fifty acres, some of them in fields and some in pine woods. It has got to have a long driveway and stone walls and a barn. The old house must overlook the river, so that I can see the tides rise and fall. And around the house I want a dozen great elm trees. The place should have a hill above the house where I can build a shop to write in, and there must be a clear, cold spring somewhere on the farm."

"Ralph," said Jim Sawyer, interrupting. "Are you pulling my leg?"

"No, of course not," my father said. "Furthermore, the

farm should be about a mile from the village, and the house
has got to be about halfway between the road and the river.
Along the drive, I want stone walls, and around the house I'd
like two acres of green lawn."

By this time, Mr. Sawyer was regarding my father with
some astonishment. "Do you know my aunts in Durham,
New Hampshire?" he asked increduously.

My father said that he didn't think so. "Why, Jim?"

"Because you have been describing almost precisely a
farm that they have just remodeled in that town. I thought
you were pulling my leg. The house was first put up in 1685,
but my aunts had it rebuilt last year. They might be persuaded
to sell it.

"It overlooks salt water," Jim Sawyer went on. "It has
elm trees, a long driveway, four miles of stone walls, two acres
of lawn, a barn, a stand of pine, a marvelous spring, plenty of
fields, and fifty acres, more or less. Are you sure that you
haven't just come from there, Ralph?"

"I have never been to Durham in my life," my father said.
"But I would like to see this place. It can't have all of those
things that you have just enumerated."

"Well, it has," Jim Sawyer maintained. "And if you can
spare one more day, we'll go up tomorrow and look at it."

My father agreed that this was a splendid idea and called
his paper to say that he was working on a terrific story in New
Hampshire and would be a day late in getting back to New
York. Newspaper reporters have not changed much in the past
fifty or sixty years.

The next morning, they took a train to Durham. The
date was May 5, 1907. Everything Jim Sawyer had said there
in the Parker House had been true. The place was one of those
rare combinations . . . a salt water farm in a college town.

Perhaps the story did grow a little with re-telling during the next forty-five years, but there was enough truth in it to make me see how lucky I had been. If my father had not met his classmate in the Parker House that night, I might have become a typical Maine character, spittin' to loo'rd and eternally talking about the wind direction. "Shiftin' a mite down to th' sou'east, ain't she? More'n likely go sou' sou'east by evenin'."

Furthermore, there would not have been a Shankhassick. There probably would have been cows, but nothing to match Nether Craig Spicy Peach. And there would have been a horse in those early days, but probably not a real biter like Charley. The salt water would have been about the same, and the winters would have been only slightly colder.

But whether we would have saved the surrey and the old Franklin and the cultivators and the hardened cement is open to question. We probably would have treasured the old trunks and *The National Geographics* and stored them in the attic, just as we have in New Hampshire. Most likely we also would have hung on to the first water pump and its rusty check valve.

However, we would have missed living in a college community. Half town and half gown, an educational center spawns an atmosphere all its own. In time, the town learns to cope with the gown, and nobody gets surprised.

I remember that once during a student campaign to elect a mythical mayor of Durham, faculty members and townspeople carefully stepped around a coffin that had been placed before the door of the U. S. Post Office.

Inside this rather elaborate container lay an undergraduate, his eyes closed, his face immobile, campaigning for the mayor's office on a commendable platform of silence. Adults hardly gave it a glance. Yet this inspired political beginner

very nearly won the election. During the contest, he was transported about the village in an ancient hearse.

While his opponents shouted and harangued groups of
students at every opportunity, the silent candidate lay quietly
in his coffin, garnering votes by the novelty of his platform.
He never spoke. Unfortunately, he was later nosed out by a
male student in female garb who campaigned on a sterling
platform of free beer for all the village inhabitants.

On the other hand, the old-fashioned, horse-drawn hearse
had been a familiar sight for many years. Since 1920, it had
exerted a powerful influence on students' imaginations. However, in 1956 it was withdrawn from circulation at the request
of several townspeople who remembered when it served a
more somber purpose.

During its heyday, the enchanting vehicle appeared at
nearly all student demonstrations. It played an important part
in countless football rallies, student mayoralty campaigns, and
outbursts of undergraduate enthusiasm each spring. Those
of us who have continued to live in Durham rather miss the
venerable wagon.

People who reside in college communities are often asked
what it is like to inhabit an area that includes more than three
thousand students. The most obvious answer is that life here
is often noisy. Most American males between the ages of
eighteen and twenty-two are addicted to gunpowder, dynamite, trumpets, group singing in the streets, and automobile
horns.

The compulsion to ignite explosives at two o'clock in the
morning appears to be an overwhelming one with undergradu-
ates. Consequently, Durham is frequently rocked at night by
the ear-shattering sound of exploding chemicals. How many
of these masterful contrivances are home-made, or how many

are purchased, is a question that has never been successfully determined by the Dean of Men. Suffice it to say, that the majority of them are of good quality, designed apparently to shake a house without removing the plaster.

Moreover, their periodic appearances seem to follow no pattern. A minor explosion, for example, takes place in the vicinity of a men's dormitory on Mill Road. Approximately twenty seconds later, fraternity row on the other side of the campus replies with a salvo that would make the U.S.S. *Missouri* envious. Then the cannonading subsides. In the meantime, however, most of us within a three-mile radius have been awakened by the concussion of the blast. About all we can do is lie silently in our beds, making succinct observations on modern youth.

In recent years, the old-time college prank has been partially replaced by a growing tendency on the part of students to discuss academic subjects late at night. A student, for instance, in one dormitory suddenly gets an urge to talk over the next day's physics examination with a friend in a fraternity house four hundred feet away. The resulting conversation becomes a matter of public knowledge.

In fairness to the student body here, however, it must be admitted that Durham residents often sleep through the entire night without being awakened. Collegiate enthusiasms are sporadic, unrehearsed, and sometimes downright droll.

When former President Truman came to town during one of his last campaigns while he was still in the White House, a carload of students pushed their way into the procession as it moved along Main Street. Two or three Secret Service men turned pale, and State Police officers nudged the car to the curb.

This was satisfactory to everybody, but there was more

to come. As the Presidential car passed a fraternity house farther up the street, some unsung genius let go with a firecracker. The resulting bang was highly successful and had a powerful influence on the Secret Service. Judging that their interests could best be served by removing the President from the scene as quickly as possible, they ordered the caravan to pass by an assembly of students and faculty members which had been waiting to greet him. This was not satisfactory to anybody, and the town went heavily Republican in the next election.

The college prank, except when it is downright destructive, is often ingenious, admirable, and amusing. The engineering problem, for example, connected with hoisting a wagon to the top of the University flagpole has occupied the attention of students for many years. A full-sized, old-fashioned buggy dangling in the air seventy-five feet above the campus is an impressive stunt at any time.

Perhaps the most cunningly devised prank ever seen in Durham came to light one morning in the nineteen twenties. During the night before, some students with a highly developed sense of the dramatic, arranged their props on the lawn in front of the administration building. In the course of contriving their masterpiece, they had borrowed liberally from the town of Durham, the biology laboratory, and the department of animal husbandry.

Arising students and townspeople were greeted by the sight of the old horse-drawn roadscraper reposing on the campus. On one side of the tongue stood a skeleton of a cow. Its pulling partner was an equally impressive skeleton of a horse. In the ancient metal seat sat the determined skeleton of a man, a whip in his bony fingers, lashing his emaciated steeds on. The only clue to the identity of those who perpetrated the prank was the genius-like touch that had been added apparently at the last moment. On the bald cranium of the bony driver rested a freshman beany cap, bearing the numerals of that year's freshman class.

However, not all of the comedy of a college town is generated by the student body. Deans and faculty members have contributed mightily to the cause. There was Dean Charles Pettee, for one, whom we all remember with affection. He had come over from Hanover when the State University was first located in Durham, and he continued to influence the village until a few years ago.

Prior to 1910, water for the townspeople was obtained from individual wells and springs, and was forced into taps by various contrivances and pumps which were understood only by E. A. Prescott, the village plumber. This was the same man who left his mark at Shankhassick with a fifty-foot water tower, and the pump which we still have in the barn.

But after 1910, individual water systems in the center of the village gradually began to give way to a privately-owned utility, sired by Dean Pettee. And though this estimable gentleman has since passed on, he bequeathed to his heirs and assigns, and to the village proper, a system of pipes that still defies detection several decades later.

The dean's private water works grew from a deep well and a few lengths of second-hand pipe into a meandering, uncharted system that not only kept the village more or less supplied with water, but also produced a kind of legend in the making.

Even when there was no water in the faucets, people could not help but applaud the dean's admirable intentions and his undoubted worth in supplying a utility not otherwise available. His parsimonious approach to new pipe and his uncanny ability to remember where it had been laid were both targets for village wit. The burden of relocating the pipe once it had been buried fell solely on his shoulders because of his commendable habit of employing student labor for trenching operations. By the time it became necessary to get at the pipe again, the students would have long since left town. It was assumed, and subsequent events have borne this out, that the dean never made a map of his system, but depended instead on a wonderfully developed intuitive sense of sniffing out buried pipe.

Whenever one of these clogged or a new connection had to be made, the dean would trot down from his college office with a student and shovel in tow, and quickly survey the suspected area. Then he would squint along a stone wall until he found the particular rock he was looking for, and having located it, he would line it up with an elm tree on the far side of the street and take ten paces backwards. Here he would get down and feel the earth—some say he actually smelled it—and then beckon to the student. "Dig right here," he would say confidently. The student would make the earth fly, and in a short time his shovel would strike pipe. Whereupon, the dean would issue further instructions and trot back to his office in the administration building.

It was a method that was cheaper than having maps made, and it worked admirably until the dean died. When that happened, however, the village was left in a bit of a muddle. In recent years, an electric mine detector has helped some, but at best it has been no match for the dean. For one thing, it cannot tell the difference between pipe and an old horse shoe.

On the other hand, the dean's reputation for close-fistedness was associated with his water system and not with his general character, as hundreds of grateful graduates can attest. He knew the worth of a dollar and made no bones about it.

It was hard to put much over on Dean Pettee. As a consequence, legends grew up around him. One of these, possibly apocryphal, concerned the time he blew up the pump house from which the village water was supplied. According to the story, the dean had come down from his office one afternoon and stopped in at the well to see how things were going. As he hastened up to the little pump house, he detected an odor of gasoline.

The dean discovered that the engine had stopped, and a closer inspection revealed that its gasoline tank had sprung a leak. As a result, almost five gallons, by the dean's estimate, had flowed down into the well.

Remember now, the dean was not one to take this loss lightly. Five gallons of gasoline represented a respectable amount of money and was worth salvaging. Moreover, the dean figured that the gasoline was presumably floating on top of the water. If he could think of some way to siphon it back up, he would be that much to the good. The first thing to do, though, was to get a good look at it.

So he lighted a lantern that was handy and lowered it down the well on a rope. And just when he was getting his first glimpse of all that gasoline on top of the water, there was a flash and explosion, followed by a substantial rush of hot air. The dean went up through the top of the pump house and landed ten feet away in a hay field. Parts of the house and the pump went considerably farther.

Well, it looked bad for the dean. He lay there, unmoving, his clothes in tatters, his hair singed, and his eyes closed.

Friends and neighbors came running from every direction, drawn by the shattering noise of ignited gasoline. They gazed down sorrowfully at the ragged, seared form. One of them expressed the general concensus. "He's gone, boys, I guess." The others agreed. The job was now up to the undertaker.

Then one of the neighbors, Frank Morrison, stepped forward and gazed hard at the dean. He shook his head dubiously.

"Hold on a minute," he cried, struck by a sudden thought. "I ain't so sure that he's done for." He looked around at the crowd and added, "There's one good way to tell. Anybody got a penny?"

Somebody produced a copper from his pocket. Frank took the coin and, stooping down, laid it carefully in the dean's burnt, outstretched hand.

For a moment or two, nothing happened. Then, slowly at first, the burnt fingers began to close. A tiny trace of a smile broke over the damaged face. Finally, the fist snapped shut, and a grateful sigh came from the twisted lips.

Frank stood up and nodded reassuringly. "The dean's all right, boys," he said, "let's get him down to the doctor's."

There were other titans in the local legends, too. Men who for one reason or another became permanently fixed in the memories of their fellow townspeople. Sam Runlett, who presided over the Post Office for many years, is remembered best for originating the most devastating judgment ever pronounced by one man against another. In assessing the effectiveness of a certain neighbor, he called him "the only stillborn child that ever lived."

There was also Charlie Wentworth. Charlie was the station agent for the Boston and Maine railroad for thirty or forty years.

Actually, he was more than a railroad employee. He was an institution. In time, his name became synonymous with that of the B&M. He was noted far and wide for certain characteristics that endeared him to the villagers but undoubtedly exasperated the railroad. Among them was a noble disregard for system and order. He treated both of these with magnificent disdain, and though the road frequently tried to change him, it never succeeded. To the very end of his life he reveled in a chaos of old telegrams, waybills, Sunday newspapers, insurance forms and letters from the railroad, asking for explanations.

These last always amused him. He wrote the answers in pencil and sent them along to the Boston office. His handwriting was atrocious. During his long tenure, various assistants came to him as boys and went away men. If he accomplished nothing else, his name would be honored in local history as solid proof that one determined man can more than hold his own against a heartless corporation.

Charlie's relationship with supervisory personnel was remarkable. He treated them with a good-humored tolerance,
and some pity. Like all large companies, the B&M went
through a good many reforms in accounting and clerical pro-
cedure during Mr. Wentworth's time. As a rule, he ignored
them.

At one time, the railroad got pretty excited about effect-
ing some new economies in freight handling and tried to pass
them down the line. The experts in the Boston office felt it
would be a good idea if station agents throughout the hinter-
land enforced the rule that persons receiving shipments in
freight cars clean them out before turning them back to the
railroad.

Charlie took this in stride until the day that a carload
of sheep arrived at the siding. In due course, the receivers
came down from a farm that was twenty miles distant and un-
loaded their live freight. Then they departed, leaving the car
pretty well littered up. The following day, the agent banged
the doors shut and dispatched it back to its place of origin.

The car had traveled but seven miles to the neighboring
city of Dover when a freight supervisor cast an eagle eye at its in-
terior. His indignation was prompt and official. He addressed
his communication to Charles Wentworth, Agent, Durham.
As forcefully as he could, he drew attention to the recent
ruling regarding freight cars. He suggested that Mr. Wentworth, acting as a representative of the line, call back the
offenders who had received the sheep and make them clean up
the mess. He expressed a desire for an early answer.

Charlie took his stubby, soft pencil from behind his ear
and wrote back a more or less unintelligible reply to the office
that the lads who had bought the sheep lived a long way back

in the woods, without telephone service, and it seemed unlikely that they would be willing to undertake the chore for the sake of the B&M. He put this on a late afternoon train for Dover.

The answer was on his desk when he came in the next day. The Dover official deplored the situation referred to in the recent communication. He wrote, moreover, that the freight car was still on the siding where it would remain until something was done. At the same time the official again took this opportunity to mention that the condition of said car was intolerable. In fact, he wrote, it contained one dead sheep in a corner.

Upon receiving it, Mr. Wentworth shook silently in his chair for a few minutes, as was his wont when pleased, and began his reply. He explained the circumstances again, and then added a postscript:

"I would be very much interested," he wrote, "to hear whether in the interests of efficiency and economy for the railroad you have been able to salvage that pelt."

As far as Charlie was concerned, that ended the exchange, but somehow news of it got abroad. It traveled the length and breadth of the state and into Maine and down into Massachusetts. For months after, strange, grinning faces would appear at doors of railroad mail cars, cabooses and engine cabs. Invariably, they had one question to ask of the Durham station agent.

"Hey, Charlie," their voices would call: "Were they able to salvage that pelt?"

Charlie's railroad life was complicated by the fact that he operated a substantial insurance business on the side. There was a good reason for this. For most of his adult years, he also served the village as town clerk. And in the State of New

Hampshire, the town clerk performs a multitude of duties. He licenses the dogs, for one thing. He likewise issues permits for the registration of automobiles. There is a direct connection between insurance and car owners, as Charlie perceived when still a young man. Consequently, he carried on a good deal of business without moving from his railroad desk.

This roll-top affair also served as the nerve center for various other enterprises. In addition to automobile insurance, Charlie carried on a lively trade in protecting houses, barns and sheds against loss through fire. At this desk, too, the rather negligible accounting system of a Sunday newspaper agency was maintained. During his lifetime, it was possible to make one visit to the railroad station and transact the following business: Buy a ticket to Miami, register a car, insure it, along with the house and barn, order the Sunday paper for the next ten years, send a telegram to San Francisco, obtain a license for any sized dog, collect any telegrams that had come in during the past forty-eight hours, and hear a couple of very droll stories. It was a process that required an hour or more, but most of the villagers felt well rewarded.

Occasionally, however, somebody would move in from the city and attempt to shorten the ritual of doing business at the railroad station. Some tried, none succeeded. Faculty wives at the University were especially unsympathetic toward a system that kept them waiting outside in the car for an hour or more.

One who had spectacular failure in this line was an overzealous matron who tired of watching the trains go by while her husband was obtaining an auto permit inside the station. At the end of an hour, she decided to go in after him. Her eye immediately fell on her husband who was bent over double beside the telegraph key, gasping for air. At the roll-top desk,

Charlie was shaking gently to and fro, his mouth open in noiseless mirth. They continued this way for some moments before noting her presence. When they did, her husband straightened up as best he could, wiped a tear from his eye and then fell to whooping again. All he could manage to gasp to Mr. Wentworth were the improbable words: "Two midgets, did you say?" He fell to slapping his thigh.

His spouse's indignation was colossal. To discover her husband doing nothing better than listening to an apparently inconsequential story about two persons of very small stature while she waited in the car was almost more than she could bear. She fairly yelped her outrage. She harangued her husband. She threatened him. She gave him a piece of her mind.

When she had come to the end, Charlie looked up at the man sternly. "Are you legally married to this woman, sir?" he asked.

The husband nodded his head. Charlie turned back to the application that he had been filling out and scribbled for a moment. Then, still ignoring the woman, he turned to the man and shook his head sorrowfully. "Well, then, God help you, sir!" he exclaimed feelingly and handed him his permit.

Whenever the pressure from the head office in Boston became too great, Mr. Wentworth would retire behind the bulwark of his incomprehensible handwriting and wait it out. Among some of the railroad's personnel, there was a strong suspicion that he used this weapon to a fare-thee-well. Most of his communications were written in pencil on odd scraps of paper. After all, it is pretty hard to condemn what a man writes when you aren't sure what he has said. During his lifetime, however, this ruse saved him from the railroad's wrath more than once.

Like a good many New Hampshiremen, Charlie had the

remarkable ability to carry a joke through with a straght face. His eyes might occasionally betray him, but never his mouth. This trait served him well at the ticket window, for he had a deep suspicion of the road's banking facilities. In the Durham station, these consisted of a battered old safe that had been cracked three or four times by itinerant burglars. Its door was flared out from successive explosions, and the lock bore the marks of intense heat. Not once, however, did the thieves find enough to make their nocturnal labors worthwhile. On one occasion, they swiped the agent's rubbers which were locked away inside the safe, and the next time, they stole his gloves. If they ever did find any swag, it never amounted to more than a dollar or two.

This precaution about leaving money in the station overnight sometimes caused embarrassment when the ticket window opened for business. One morning, for instance, a woman asked to buy a ticket to Boston. In those days, railroad travel was cheaper, and the cost of riding to the Hub was around two dollars. She drew a twenty dollar bill from her bag and presented it in payment.

Knowing full well that he didn't have enough cash on hand to change it, Charlie picked up the bill and examined it carefully. Then he looked the woman straight in the eye. "Sorry, ma'am," he said, his voice tinged with suspicion, "I guess I can't sell you a ticket this morning. That bill, unfortunately, isn't legal tender." He handed it back to her.

Immediately, the customer's mouth fell open in indignation and surprise. Then she exploded. "Of course, that's legal tender! Whoever heard of such a thing?"

Feigning great sorrow, Charlie shook his head. "No, ma'am," he said. "Legal tender means that you have the exact number of dollars, quarters, dimes and pennies for a ticket to

Boston. If you had that, we'd be allowed to take your money."
He brushed his small, sandy mustache. "It's a railroad regulation now," he said, "and they won't let us take anything except legal tender."

Naturally, the woman raised the temperature of the station considerably, but Charlie was firm. He went on to point
out that a rule was a rule, and he wasn't the one to break it.
Eventually, the train came, and the woman got aboard and
bought her ticket from a conductor who had not heard of
the regulation concerning legal tender. When she got to Boston, she reported this odd incident to the management at the
North Station.

In due time, a communication from headquarters came
down the line to Charlie, requesting an explanation. Un-
abashed, he sat down and scribbled a reply. He spent a considerable amount of time on it, and when he was through,
even he could not say for sure what he had written. "Yes, sir,"
he gloated to his assistant, "that will do, all right. Can't read it
myself."

Its dispatch was followed the next day by its return.
Across the top of the letter was a penciled note: "You'll have
to do better than this. We can't make it out."

Charlie's eyes twinkled, and he rewrote the whole explanation. This time, it was sort of a blur of lead on a page.
"That will do it all right," he said confidently. And it did, too.
Either the railroad gave it up as a bad job, or else the management is still trying to decipher that note. Regardless of
which surmise is correct, however, in Durham legal tender to
this day means the exact change.

There were perhaps a dozen other men in the village who
obtained the stature of Charlie Wentworth, Dean Pettee, and
Sam Runlett. Inevitably, time has added to their stature, too.

Since their era, both the town and college have undergone a
revolution. Deans no longer smell out lost pipe. Charlie
Wentworth's town clerk's job has been taken over by a crisp
young lady who can type several hundred words a minute. The
railroad station has been abandoned. Some advanced thinkers
are even toying with the idea of a traffic light at the corner
of Main and Madbury.

But the memory of those characters makes me more glad
than ever that my father met his classmate at the Parker
House that night in 1907. Castine, Maine might have been
able to produce a Charlie Wentworth or a Sam Runlett, but
certainly not a Dean Pettee. These were pure New Hampshiremen, totally unconcerned with the direction of the wind or
whether it was shiftin' down to the sou'east.

Frequently at social gatherings here, the men who have
watched the slow transition of the village during the past fifty
years get off in a corner by themselves and lament the change.
We kick the topic around a bit, and then somebody says, "Do
you remember the time . . . ?" and another legend comes to
light.

Maybe we are only fooling ourselves. Age may have something to do with our nostalgia for the old days. A German lady
who came to Durham just after World War I as the bride of
an American doughboy possibly supplied the answer for us.
One morning, she and Brad McIntire, the municipal judge,
were standing on the sidewalk in front of a local clothing store.

Brad told a couple of stories about Frank Morrison and
Dean Pettee and Professor Curry, who transported his donkey
about in the back seat of a Crane Simplex. The judge be-
moaned the fact that the old-timers were gone, and there
seemed to be no real characters coming along to take their
places. Part of the picturesqueness of the old village had been

lost forever, he felt. The two of them went on in this vein for some time, but then the German lady had a thought.

"Brad," she said with a sudden flash of insight. "Brad, perhaps now ve is de characters."

And perhaps we are.